D1682914

BRAGGING RIGHTS

The Dallas-Houston Rivalry
Based on Interviews with Leaders from Every Sector in Both Cities

Carolyn Kneese & John DeMers
with Lynn Ashby

bright sky press
HOUSTON, TEXAS

A Note from the Editors

To create Bragging Rights, Carolyn Kneese and John DeMers invited notable citizens of Dallas and Houston to contribute their perspective on their city or both cities by answering an open-ended questionnaire. From these responses, John DeMers crafted pieces quoting the contributors; in some cases contributors chose to write their own pieces, but in every case these responses are directly generated from the questions we asked. The pieces we have included should in no way be construed as complete reflections of the attitudes of the men and women who so generously agreed to participate in our survey. It is our hope that the combination of their unique perspectives and Lynn Ashby's informed overviews will leave you with a better understanding of what creates the powerful civic pride in both these cities.

bright sky press
HOUSTON, TEXAS

2365 Rice Blvd., Suite 202
Houston, Texas 77005

Copyright © 2014
No part of this book may be reproduced in any form or by any electronic or mechanical means, including information storage and retrieval devices or systems, without prior written permission from the publisher, except that brief passages may be quoted for reviews.

ISBN: 978-1-939055-62-0

10 9 8 7 6 5 4 3 2 1

Library of Congress Cataloging-in-Publication Data on file with publisher.

These essays were collected with the written permission of the contributors in whole or in part based on a series of questions. Bright Sky Press reserves the right to edit collected responses in a manner that best adds value to the whole of the work.

Editorial Direction: Lucy Herring Chambers
Editor: Eva J. Freeburn
Designer: Marla Y. Garcia

Many thanks to Lauren Patterson for her capable and cheerful assistance during the interviewing phase of *Bragging Rights*, and to Kate Sanford for her diligent assistance during the final stages of this project.

Printed in Canada through Friesens

WE OFFER THIS COLLECTION OF OPINIONS AS A TRIBUTE TO THOSE WHO LOVE AND SERVE THEIR RESPECTIVE CITIES

I-45

Rarely a week goes by that someone doesn't ask me: What is the difference between Dallas and Houston? Although I'm not a self-appointed authority, let me fill you in a bit as to why someone might ask that question. Throughout my life I've been blessed to have lived in both cities. By 2009 I had residences in both cities, but today only some of my belongings remain in Dallas…awaiting a possible return? Unlike me, most people who grow up in one or the other city tend to stay there. And, interestingly, many newcomers to one city tell me that they have never been to the other.

Dallas and Houston—only 250 miles apart on I-45 yet distinctly unique. With my heart in both places, I have always believed that they should celebrate their differences; a great world city is characterized by its distinctive culture. But I still wonder *exactly what makes these two cities so reputably different* and *how did they become so extraordinary?* Many cities have the same amenities, so I realize it is the people—Dallasites and Houstonians—who make their burgs so remarkable.

Dallas or Houston? I can't answer the question. So to illuminate all of us, we've interviewed eighty personalities about their beloved city. Here are the voices of Dallas and Houston sharing personal perspective on their particular culture, society, business and hometown life.

We'll leave it to you to decide who gets *Bragging Rights!*

CAROLYN KNEESE

BRAGGING RIGHTS
The Dallas-Houston Rivalry

TABLE OF CONTENTS

THE LEGACY
BIRTH OF TWO CITIES
LYNN ASHBY *9*

THE PEOPLE
01 *BUSINESS* *21*
02 *SOCIETY & PHILANTHROPY* *49*
03 *WORSHIP* *63*
04 *ARTS & CULTURE* *77*
05 *MEDICINE* *91*
06 *EDUCATION* *105*
07 *ARCHITECTURE* *121*
08 *REAL ESTATE* *137*
09 *RESTAURANTS* *151*
10 *SPORTS* *165*
11 *MEDIA* *179*

THE PROMISE
THE FUTURE OF DALLAS AND HOUSTON
LYNN ASHBY *195*

SOURCES *207*

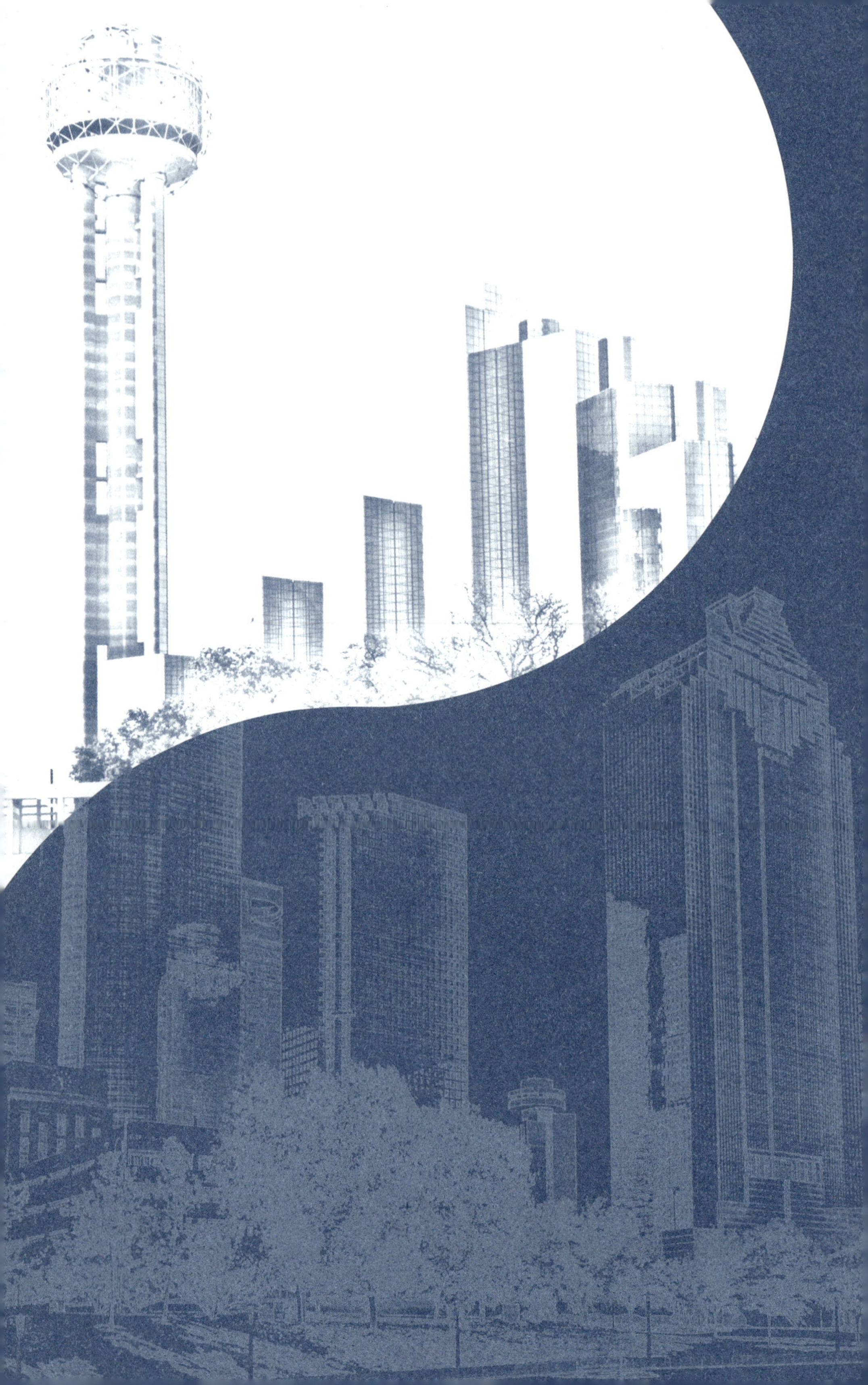

THE LEGACY
BIRTH OF TWO CITIES

LYNN ASHBY

Dallas and Houston get along like brothers—Cain and Abel. True, at first glance they seem much the same. Both are large Texas cities filled with people from somewhere else. Stand on any major street corner in either place and you can't tell the difference: Best Buy, Whataburger, CVS and there's even a Galleria (Houston's is bigger). Same governor and U.S. Senators. The billboards and license plates are identical. It might be argued that, while Houston and Dallas are their Christian names, Texas is the family name. Yet this is more than two squabbling siblings. This is big-time competition for jobs, new companies, airline routes (Dallas has more), and bragging rights in sports and barbeque.

Let's start at the beginning. Unlike most cities, Houston knows exactly when it was founded. The Allen Brothers—Augustus Chapman Allen and John Kirby Allen from New York State—paid just over $1.40 per acre for 6,642 acres of land along Buffalo Bayou, and on August 30, 1836, the brothers ran an advertisement in the *Telegraph and Texas Register* for the "Town of Houston." It would become the "great interior commercial emporium of Texas," as ships from New York and New Orleans could sail up Buffalo Bayou to its door.

"There is no place in Texas more healthy, having an abundance of excellent spring water, and enjoying the sea breeze in all its freshness." Ads were run in German newspapers touting the glories of Houston. In Hamburg, or maybe Bremen, I found some pamphlets that had been passed around the town back then. They showed Houston with snow-capped mountains in the background. Ski the Heights. Thus the Allen Brothers started a tradition for Houston developers that continues to this very day: They lied.

Houston was laid out by two other brothers, newspaper editors Gail and Thomas Borden, which explains all our misspelled street names (Labranch-LaBranch) and misidentified streets (the Southwest Freeway is actually US 59, the West Loop is Loop 610 West, and there is no such thing as the Katy Freeway—it's I-10 West). Our major streets—Main, Fannin, etc.—were laid out to run northeast southwest so that the houses could catch the prevailing Gulf breezes. The Bordens plotted Texas Avenue, which was the western edge of the city, to be fourteen Longhorn steers—or 100 feet—wide to accommodate cattle drives. Most of the other streets were eighty feet wide. Incidentally, Gail Borden soon figured out that journalism didn't pay worth a damn, invented milk and made a fortune.

In January 1837, when Francis R. Lubbock arrived on the *Laura*, the small steamship that first reached Houston, he found the bayou choked with branches and the town almost invisible. Actually, the ship went right past the village and later turned around. Muddy footprints on the bayou's bank led them to the "great interior commercial emporium of Texas." At that time, January 1, 1837, the town was made up of twelve residents and one log cabin.

The Allen Brothers had named their town after Sam Houston

and persuaded the Texas Congress to designate the site as the temporary capital of the new Republic of Texas. The village's first (of many) booms was under way: four months later there were 1,500 people and 100 houses. The Congress first met in Houston on May 1, 1837, but couth didn't catch on along the bayous. By 1839, the town was infamous for drunkenness, dueling, brawling, prostitution and profanity. The early settlers used lumber to build frame houses, ditches for drainage and pigs to clean the streets. Yellow fever struck periodically—nine times between 1839 and 1867. The 1839 epidemic killed about 12% of the population.

John James Audubon visited the town and later wrote, "We approached the President's mansion, wading in water above our ankles." He noted that the mansion was a dirty and muddy hut and that the Capitol roof leaked. The mansion's inhabitant didn't fare much better. Alexis de Toqueville, French author of *Democracy in America*, after meeting Sam Houston, said, "He is 'one of the unpleasant consequences of popular sovereignty.'"

Consider a fellow named Charles Hedenberg who persuaded an uncle living in New Jersey to come to Houston and set up a carriage shop in the 1830s. The uncle arrived one morning and transferred his bags to his nephew's business, Hedenberg and Vedder. Charles was quite busy at the time, so he suggested that his uncle go over to the Capitol and watch Congress in action. The uncle agreed and went to the Capitol, whereupon he heard gunshots. He rushed to a hallway just in time to see Algernon Thompson, a Senate clerk, being carted off. Thompson had been severely wounded by another clerk. The uncle had seen enough of Texas government in action, so he left the Capitol and walked down the west side of Main Street.

As he passed the Round Tent Saloon, inside, one Texian soldier shot another. The wounded soldier staggered out and almost fell on the New Jerseyian. He ran across the street and arrived at John Carlos' Saloon. Just then a man fell out of the saloon with his bowels protruding from a huge wound made by a Bowie knife. The newcomer raced back to his nephew's store and asked, "Charley, have you sent my trunks to the house?"

"No, Uncle. Not yet."

"Well, do not send them. Get me a dray so I can at once take them to the boat that leaves for Galveston this afternoon."

"Why, Uncle, what do you mean? You have seen nothing; have not had time to look at the town."

"Charley," said the uncle, "I have seen enough. I wish to return home immediately. I do not wish to see any more of Texas." With that, he left, never to return.

WHAT'S IN A NAME

Meantime, to the north, nothing was happening. It wasn't until nearly twenty years after Houston was birthed, that on February 2, 1856, Dallas was granted a town charter during the regular session of the Sixth Texas Legislature. Before that date, Caddo Indians had roamed the area. Otherwise, what became the crown jewel of north Texas was a slightly rolling, windy wasteland. John Neely Bryan came through in 1839 looking for a spot to start a trading post. A ford in the Trinity River was near some Indian trails. Bryan also knew that the planned Preston Trail (today's Preston Road) was to run nearby, and that's where he built his post.

After Bryan surveyed the area, he went home to Arkansas; but while there, back in Texas a treaty was signed removing all Indians from northern Texas. Bryan returned in November 1841 to find that half of his customers, the Indians, had left. Ever the clever fellow, he decided that, instead of creating a trading post, he would establish a permanent settlement, which he founded that same November 1841. Thus Bryan, like the Allen Brothers in Houston, turned a lemon into a lemonade stand.

Dallas is named either for U.S. Vice President George M. Dallas; his brother, Commodore Alexander J. Dallas; or Joseph Dallas, a local resident. None of them made any difference to Texas or to any other place. If Big D was going to become a major city, it should have been named after one of our heroes. No Dallas Cowboys. We could cheer for the Bowie Knives or the Crockett Coonskin Caps.

Near the small town, one of those utopian share-the-wealth colonies was set up with French, Belgian, Swiss and German settlers among others. They called their new home La Reunion, and it was a bust. In the late 1850s many of them moved to Dallas, giving the village a sudden infusion of skilled European craftsmen: brick-makers, cabinetmakers, tailors, milliners, brewers, artists and musicians. On July 8, 1860, a fire spread to a number of downtown buildings and destroyed them. Blame fell on slaves and Northern abolitionists; three slaves were hanged, and two Iowa preachers were whipped and run out of town. In 1861 Dallas voted 741 to 237 to secede from the Union.

COMING OF AGE

A wise man (me) once said, "Houston got the port, San Antonio got the Alamo and Fort Worth got the trains. All Dallas got was brains." Dallas County is one of the rare counties in Texas that has never had a working oil well. However, the town attracted young men, such as Robert Lee Thornton who, as a seven-year-old, learned to pick a bale of cotton a day. He occasionally attended school until the ninth grade. Thornton became a store clerk, and eventually a traveling candy salesman. Long story short, he moved to Dallas, started a financial institution, became a pillar of the community and was elected mayor. His story was not that unique in Big D. It grew from that wannabe trading post, up there on the high plains next to nowhere (except Fort Worth), to a financial and technical center for much of the state's oil industry, banking and insurance, because of mental skill, ambition and simple animal cunning.

By 1900 the city was well on its way to fame and fortune—the leading drug, book, jewelry and wholesale liquor market in the Southwest. It was also leading in the commerce of cotton, grain and even buffalo, and led the world in manufacture of saddlery. It is not clear just why Dallas was so big in buffalos hides and leather, but it was. The town slowly moved from an agricultural center to what it is today: the business of Dallas was business—banking, insurance, retailing and white-collar oil jobs. It still didn't have any oil fields to call its own, but in 1930 C.M. "Dad" Joiner struck oil 100 miles east of Dallas. The East Texas Oil Fields were the largest petroleum deposit in the world at the time, and Dallas became its office. Dallas began its still-shiny reputation as the cultural and fashion center of not only Texas but also the entire Southwest with Neiman Marcus (1907), SMU (1907) and Highland Park (1907).

In the early 1930s Texas began planning for its Centennial, and there was a fight over which city would host the celebrations. Dallas landed the festivities due to the work of the aforementioned Robert Lee Thornton. To this day the State Fair of Texas (it's *not* the Texas State Fair), remains the biggest state fair in the nation. The Cotton Bowl also wound up in Dallas, built in 1930 on the Fair Park grounds to take the place of a wooden football stadium. It was called the Fair Park Stadium and didn't become the Cotton Bowl until 1936 after Dallas grabbed that annual New Year's Day game. In the 1940s the stadium's size was greatly increased to 75,504 to accommodate the fans who turned out to see SMU halfback and Heisman Trophy recipient Doak Walker. The stadium was unofficially branded "The House That Doak Built." Not only did Dallas outsmart the rest of Texas in landing the State Fair and the Cotton Bowl, but in 1914 Dallas was selected as the site for the Federal Reserve Bank for the region.

Since Dallas's founding, the town's population grew rapidly but, unlike Houston, it saw no local oil boom, no port opening nor any yellow fever decimation. By 1860 the village's population was 678, including ninety-seven blacks. The headcount went from 3,000 in early 1872 to more than 7,000 in September of the same year. Through growth and annexation of Oak Cliff, by 1890 Little D became Big D, having the largest population in Texas with 38,067 people. Indeed, for many years it was the biggest city in the nation not on a navigable waterway until Phoenix surpassed it in 2000 and San Antonio in 2010.

The 1920 census showed Dallas had become a small city with a population of 158,976, making that former trading post (and buffalo hide capital of the world) the 42nd largest city in the nation. After a disastrous flood in 1908, Oak Cliff and Dallas were connected by the Houston Street Viaduct, at the time the longest concrete structure in the world. Following WWI, the city gained another title: with 13,000 members, the Dallas chapter of the Ku Klux Klan was the largest chapter in Texas, some 75,000 citizens greeted "Klan Day" at the 1923 State Fair.

We can pretty well speed past the 1940s and 50s in Dallas as it continued to grow only slightly slower than its civic boosterism. World War II saw most of Texas untouched; except after the heavy cruiser USS *Houston* was sunk in the western Pacific in February 1942, the citizens of Houston purchased enough war bonds for the construction of a new *Houston* as well as for a light aircraft carrier, the USS *San Jacinto*. The city also enlisted 1,000 Houston volunteers who served in the Navy. With cheap land and good weather, air bases sprang up everywhere, including in Grand Prairie next to Dallas and in the empty fields just south of Houston. Our major Army bases also gave hundreds of thousands of young Americans a taste of Texas, and after the war many returned for good.

WHAT MADE H-TOWN FAMOUS

If Big D was getting bigger, its sibling to the south was booming. Even through the capital of the Republic of Texas was lost to a village named Waterloo, later renamed Austin, General Houston's little town roared on. The Civil War drew close with the Union conquest of Galveston and the attempted invasion at the Battle of Sabine Pass. The first railroad in Texas, the Buffalo Bayou, Brazos and Colorado Railway (BBB&C), began running twenty-nine miles from Harrisburg (now a part of Houston) to Stafford's Point (now Stafford) in September 1853.

Dallas, as noted, was the largest city in the nation not on a navigable waterway, but it wasn't for lack of trying. Indeed, one reason John Neely Bryan chose his spot on the North Texas prairie for a trading post was because he thought the Trinity River had possibility for navigation to the Gulf. (But we must remember, in 1877, Bryan was committed to the State Lunatic Asylum where he died.) In 1852, James A. Smith built a flatboat, loaded it with cotton bales and left Dallas. In four months, he had only gone seventy miles. The rest of the cotton was shipped by wagon to Houston. In 1867, a boat left Galveston, and sure enough it arrived in Dallas—one year later. In the 1890s, a group of Dallas businessmen formed the Trinity River Navigation Company looking forward to creating the Port of Dallas, but the river proved unreliable as a waterway. Still, highway bridges crossing over the Trinity River—including I-10—were built high enough for big ships to pass under. They never came.

The Port of Houston was easier. Buffalo Bayou was dredged, and on November 10, 1914, that sleepy fishing village on the bayou was opened to the high seas. The wonderful combination of what became one of the largest petro-chemical installations in the world and the Port proved that oil and water do mix. Just as in Dallas, the "awl bidness" brought Houston the white collars—headquarters, offices, accountants and lots of lawyers. But there was another change that helped boost the city. *The Harris County Historical Society's Guidebook* opens with, "Our story begins in 1922 when the city's first air conditioning was installed in the Rice Hotel cafeteria. Before that, Houston was totally unlivable." Indeed, social scientists say the boom in Houston was not because of oil but of air conditioning. The only bump on the road during that time came on August 23, 1917, when the Camp Logan Riots erupted. Black soldiers, new to the town and resentful of the segregation laws, rioted. Black soldiers and white policemen were killed. Afterwards a number of the soldiers were court-martialled and hanged.

When it comes to outlaws: advantage Dallas. In the 1870s, gunslingers, gamblers, robbers and highwaymen were common in the town. Belle Starr began her adventures in Dallas as a dance hall singer and dancer, and later sold stolen horses and harbored outlaws. Doc Holliday went to Dallas for his health, and opened a dentist's office, but soon turned to gambling. In 1875, he killed a man and left town. Sam Bass robbed four trains in two months during the spring of 1878. Three months later, Bass was killed in an ambush near Round Rock. Later, two world-famous Dallasites would appear in the historical line-up: Bonnie and Clyde. On the police blotter Houston finishes a poor second out of two with only a couple of tainted developers who never spent a day in prison.

At the end of World War II, Houston began forming the Texas Medical Center, requiring all institutions to be either not-for-profit or government operations. Over the years the Center's fame and size spread, partially due to the duel between heart surgeons Dr. Michael DeBakey and Dr. Denton Cooley. Today it includes twenty-one hospitals, three public health organizations, two universities, three medical schools, six nursing programs, two pharmacy schools, a dental school, eight academic and research institutions, and thirteen support organizations. It is the largest medical center on earth, and people come from everywhere to die in Houston.

By 1950 both cities were coming of age, although neither knew it. Within the City of Dallas lived 434,462 people, Houston had 596,163.

Neither ranked in the top ten among U.S. cities, neither had a major league sports franchise, nationally recognized individuals nor even a song to boast of, although "I'll Buy That Dream" included the lyrics *We'll settle down near Dallas, in a little plastic palace, it's not as crazy as you think.* And a character in "The Treasure of the Sierra Madre" was James Cody (Bruce Bennett) from Dallas. He gets killed. Houston garnered some national attention with the opening of the Shamrock Hotel on St. Patrick's Day of 1949, an event featured in the movie *Giant*. Otherwise, there was not much to notice in Texas's Twin Cities. How things would change.

Everyone knows that President John F. Kennedy said, "We choose to go to the moon in this decade and do the other things, not because they are easy, but because they are hard." He was speaking at Rice University on September 12, 1962, two and a half months before his assassination in another Texas city. What is not well known is that JFK went on to say, "Why choose this as our goal? And they may well ask why climb the highest mountain? Why, thirty-five years ago, fly the Atlantic? Why does Rice play Texas?" To this very day, no one knows why Rice plays Texas, but it's ironic that JFK made his proposal in what was to become Space City, home of the astronauts, home of AstroWorld, the major league (occasionally) baseball team, the Astros, whose home for thirty-five years was the Astrodome.

The Brothers Allen paid just over $1.40 per acre for 6,642 acres of land; today an acre at Preston and Bagby may run a bit more, but there is more to choose from. Acording to the U.S. Census Bureau, the city currently covers 656.3 square miles with 634.0 square miles of land and 22.3 square miles of water. Not to repeat myself, but it's too good a stat to let slide: You could fit New York City, Boston, Miami, San Francisco, Minneapolis and Seattle inside Houston with room to spare. The Houston-Woodlands-Sugar Land metropolitan area has a total area of 10,062 square miles; 8,929 square miles are land, while 1,133 are water. That is slightly smaller than Massachusetts and slightly larger than New Jersey. Houston's construction growth has been greatly helped by the lack of zoning—the largest city in America with such non-restrictions. As for people, the first U.S. Census in 1850 counted 2,396 in the city and 4,688 in Harris County. That doubled in ten years to 4,845 for the city and almost doubled with 9,070 for the county. In six of the nine U.S. Censuses from 1850 to 1930, Houston's population doubled. In 2012, the city held 2,160,821 with 4,180,894 in the county and 6,086,538 for this ten-county region. About half of the population growth in the Houston area comes from natural increase—births minus deaths—and the other half is due to people moving to the area.

HOW LITTLE D BECAME BIG

Dallas has a reputation and a certain sophistication far beyond its size. Ranking only 9th in population among all U.S. cities, everyone knows Dallas, not because of its citizens, schools or skyline, but because of Neiman's, J.R. Ewing and America's Team, the Cowboys. It still doesn't have a harbor, but it carved an airport out of the prairie that is larger than Manhattan Island and has its own ZIP code. The old line is, "If you want to go to hell you have to go through DFW." With no large military bases like San Antonio and most of West Texas, Dallas turned to making itself indispensable in the Texas business world. You've got to hand it to Dallas. Few cities have done so much with so little.

In the post-war years all of Texas boomed, and Dallas was getting its share. One advantage it had over its large brother in the Buffalo Bayou swamps was its neighbor to the west, Fort Worth. In former years the two cities competed with each other, showing a certain dis like. But as Dallas grew in population and influence, the city passed aptly named Cow Town and the competition wasn't so fierce anymore. There is no Twin Cities feeling, but together they form the Metroplex, bringing in suburbs in every direction to create a population pool larger than Houston's.

If today Dallas is best known for a TV show and football team, it burst onto the world stage on November 22, 1963, when a lone drifter named Lee Harvey Oswald assassinated President John F. Kennedy. The fact that two previous presidents had been murdered in Washington, D.C. and one in Buffalo, New York, didn't help Dallas fade the heat. The city had a reputation as a hard-nosed, right-wing, anti-JFK and anti-LBJ town. It was as though the people of Dallas had met in the Cotton Bowl and voted for the assassination. (This actually happened: A friend from Dallas was visiting New York City, talking business in an office, when an employee burst in shouting: "Now you've done it! You've killed our president!") An editorial cartoon in an Iowa newspaper summed up the nation's feeling: "Deep in the hate of Texas." It was a cheap shot, so to speak, but accurately reflected America's mood and blame game.

The town prospered despite the bad image, attracting Texas Instruments engineers, Nobel Prize recipients at University of Texas-Southwestern Medical Center at Dallas, good looking women and handsome men. The best and the brightest from north Texas, Oklahoma and Arkansas, not to mention every place else, flocked to the faceless office parks scattered around and the singles bars on McKinney Street to be a part of the fast-moving, cutting-edge scene. If success breeds success, there's a whole lot of breeding going on in Dallas.

Y2K

This brings us to the year 2000. By then, Dallas was loafers, chardonnay and Volvos. Houston was boots, hard hats and pickups. "A whiskey and trombone town," it's been called. Dallas looked northeast towards Wall Street. Houston looked—in the mirror. It speaks volumes that the biggest social event in Dallas is the Cotillion, with its famed "Texas Dip." Residents in the Bayou City live for the annual Houston Live Stock Show and Rodeo. Each city has ample reasons to be proud, but there is a small, gnawing jealousy that seeps through. Dallas has Highland Park, with its modest magnificence. Houston has River Oaks, but there is no River Oaks school district. Houston has one of the mightiest ports on Earth. Dallas's steamboats are still stuck in Trinity sandbars.

Yet each one would be less inviting, busy and prosperous without the other. Any Southwest Airline flight between Dallas and Houston is filled with lawyers carrying their tell-tale black leather boxes, commuters who can watch a Texas Rangers game in the terminal bar begin at Love Field and catch the ninth inning at Hobby. Statewide political candidates have to spend money and time in both cities, finding it difficult if not impossible to win without both. Each has something the other covets.

As Cain probably said to Abel, "Mother always liked you best."

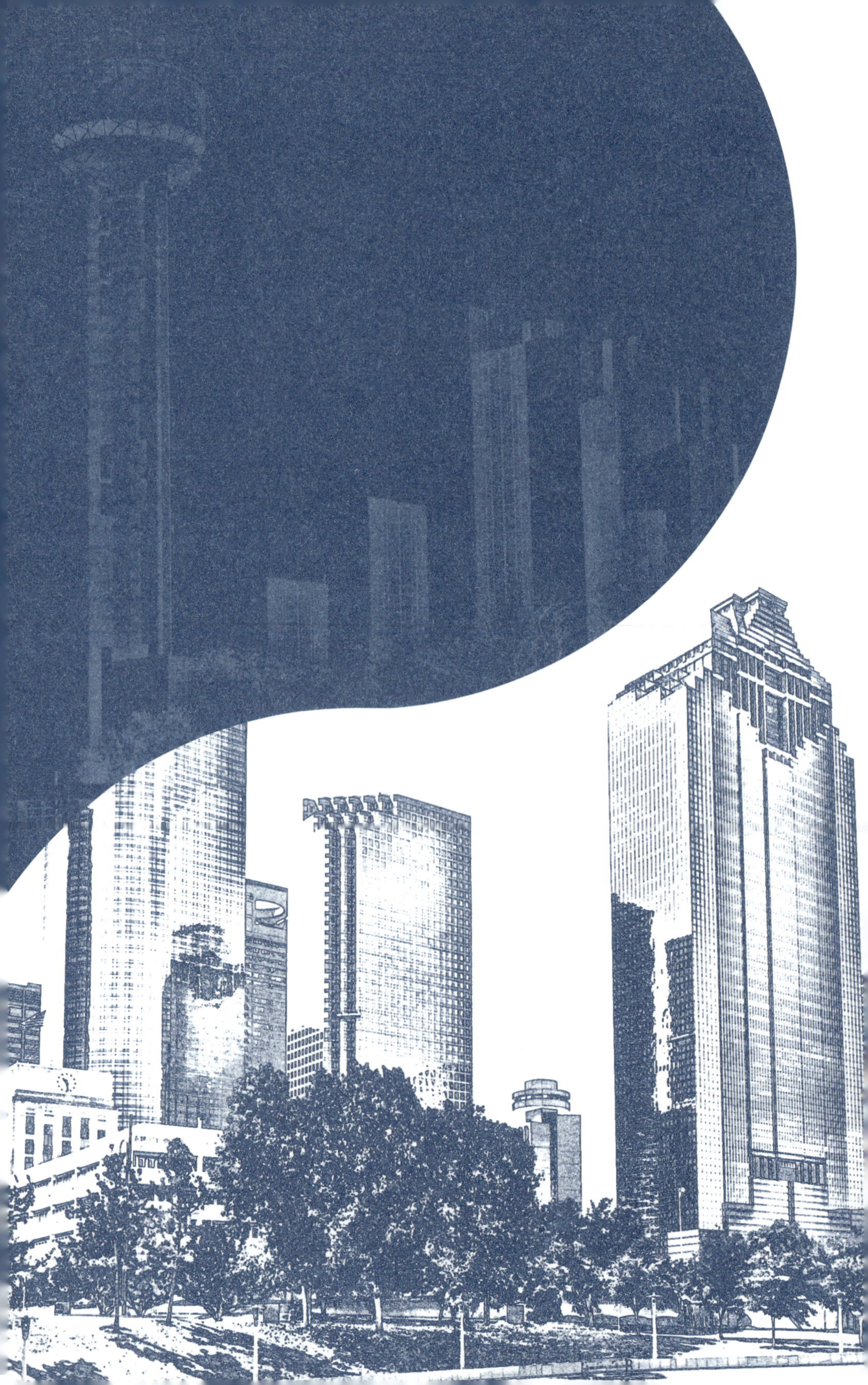

THE PEOPLE
BUSINESS

The two largest cities in Texas have diversified their economies every chance they've gotten over the decades, making each a modern metropolis with jobs in every conceivable field. To those who understand them best, however, the personalities of Houston and Dallas were formed early around answers to the simplest of questions: How do they make their money? Both cities want a lot of the same things for their citizens. But the roads they chose to travel in terms of business couldn't be more different.

In Houston today, there's no shortage of towering glass-and-steel corporate headquarters, and certainly no shortage of operas, ballets, museums and art galleries, the marks of a sophisticated city built on money and influence. Yet few are the Houstonians who let themselves forget that the two most important events in the city's history—the discovery of oil at Spindletop in 1901 and the origins of the port with the Houston Ship Channel in 1914—mark the city as a roll-up-your-sleeves, rough-and-tumble, blue-collar kind of town. Houston is a clean city that's proudest of its willingness to get its hands dirty.

The skyline of Dallas is not too different from that of its Gulf Coast sibling, yet the inhabitants of *its* glass-and-steel corporate headquarters have been different from the beginning. Oil is now an afterthought in Dallas, as recent decades have created a metropolis that has grown up around white-collar enterprises like insurance, finance and transportation. Dallasites love to "clean up nice," just like their wealthy counterparts in Houston. They simply work harder at pretending it's their birthright.

ANNISE PARKER

Mayor Parker is Houston's 61st mayor and one of only two women to hold the city's highest elected office. Parker has also spent six years as a City Council member and six years as City Controller. She is the only person in Houston history to hold the offices of council member, controller and mayor.

There is a vibrancy here that you don't feel anywhere else. If you can dream it, you can achieve it here. Houston was recently named the nation's most diverse city. Our diversity is our strength. We don't experience the racial tensions that tend to plague other major U.S. cities. There is an openness and tolerance that is different.

There was a worldwide reaction when I was elected as Houston's first openly gay mayor in 2010. Outside of Houston, people were surprised by my election. There were requests for media interviews from around the globe. I used it as an opportunity to talk about how the perception of Houston is really quite different from the reality. It's that diversity and willingness to accept that I noted above. Because of

HOUSTON: *Skyline*

Houstonians' trust and support, I have been given the best job there is. They have been more interested in my performance and what I can do for Houston than the fact that I am a lesbian.

As for Houston's most defining moments, I would select the discovery of oil at Spindletop in 1901 and the first words spoken from the moon. Houston is such an aspirational city. What other city can claim the world's largest medical center—a place where medical discoveries are made every day—the most engineers per capita or the first mission to the moon? Our city is full of dreamers who put their dreams into reality.

In addition to the world's largest medical center, we have the nation's 2nd largest theater district, a port that leads the nation in exports, the 4th largest museum district, representation from all major sporting leagues and more restaurants than any other city. In addition, we are the "coolest city" in the country, as noted by *Forbes* magazine. Dallas cannot beat that! The lifestyle here is laid back and welcoming, but we work hard and play hard.

ROBERT L. CLARKE

A native of New Mexico, Robert L. Clarke came to Houston in 1959 to attend Rice University. Except for time at Harvard Law School and in Washington as U.S. Comptroller of the Currency for President Reagan and the first President Bush, he's been in Houston ever since. Clarke is now a senior partner at Bracewell & Giuliani LLP.

Houston is as good as any, if not the best, business town you could ever have. We've had a lot of entrepreneurs who've gravitated here to start businesses or put businesses together to form something new over the years. Texas, of course, has a very favorable business climate in terms of regulation that has attracted a lot of the brightest people. There are so many new firms in Houston today that weren't here twenty or even ten years ago. And it's a better economy now than it used to be. It's so much more diversified. The Medical Center has always been important, but it's gotten bigger. The Port has always been important, but it's gotten bigger. We have an entire economy built around technology. Oil will always be central in Houston, but we're not so dependent on it today as we used to be.

Houston was an international city as far back as most of us can remember. The Port had a lot to do with that, but it has become even more international. Houston is now one of the most culturally diverse cities in this country. There's hardly any ethnic group not represented here, some in quite significant numbers, though a lot of people who aren't here don't seem to realize that yet. The Port brings in a lot of people. If you go to the Medical Center and look at the people walking down the halls, you have medical personnel and patients from all over the world. And finally, the Houston-based oil companies work in Africa, the Middle East and the North Sea. People coming to Houston for this work also contribute to the city's diversity.

During my years as Comptroller of the Currency, which meant I was the chief regulator of all nationally chartered banks, I learned something about Houston and the rest of Texas that I've never forgotten. Those were some terrible times for banks, in the late 80s and early 90s, when it was my responsibility to shut down virtually all of the large banks in Texas because they were insolvent. The contagion spread from here, and a lot of other banks were forced to close, too. It was a difficult time for them and a difficult time for me, as many of those bankers were my friends and clients. The bankers in Texas, after I closed them down, all hitched up their pants and started over. The bankers on the East Coast all asked me when the government was going to solve their problems. To me that reflected the greatest difference between Texas, Houston in particular, and what you find in other parts of the country.

I think the future of Houston is bright, if we don't get overconfident. Now that we've got the momentum, my hope is that Houston will continue to capitalize on its many advantages. If we're going to have growth, we need to keep up with it. We don't want to start going backwards instead of forward. In the last few years, we've been fortunate to have a City Council that's smart and progressive, and we have a mayor who has done a good job. Then again, she's a Rice graduate, so I'd expect her to do a good job.

HAIDAR BARBOUTI

As CEO of the Highland Village Shopping Center, Haidar Barbouti is responsible for leasing more than $150 million worth of high-end retail property. He has spent his entire career in retail real estate, with commercial property stretching from Houston to New York City.

Whenever I speak to national retail tenants, they often don't understand the cosmopolitan nature of Houston. They really do think there are horses and tumbleweed. And they're always very, very surprised by the sophistication, the wealth, the arts and the culture they find here. The Houston they meet at Highland Village is casual; it's warm-weather so you can be outside almost every day of the year. It's well-to-do and educated, with a lot of people who came here from all over the world. That last element puts us on par with the New Yorks and L.A.s of the world.

When this shopping center was built in the late 1950s, this was the edge of town, with farms beyond the railroad tracks. As the town grew westward and River Oaks filled out, this became the center of everything. In 1989 and 1990, when I first looked at the place to buy, its unique quality was being on both sides of Westheimer, the main east-west shopping artery in Houston. It had a certain Wow Factor even back then. The tenant mix was mostly local. Today they're mostly national and international.

It was obvious we could get better tenants, retailers more in keeping with the best neighborhood in town—the kind of stores these people visited when they traveled to New York or L.A. I knew that the center could only get better and that Houston could only get better. The city was coming off the oil slump, which had been more of a depression here than a recession. There were still a lot of vacancies in retail, office and residence. It was simply Houston's time.

The industries that drive our flagship retailers, places like the Apple Store and Restoration Hardware, are oil (but with natural gas playing a larger role than in the past, adding stability to the local economy), the Medical Center and the Port. The oil industry brings a lot of people here from anywhere there's oil—Indonesia, the Middle East, Africa, Brazil and Mexico. People also fly here for treatment at our Medical Center, especially in the areas of heart disease and cancer. And the Port is going to drive a lot of growth, too. As time goes on, we're going to go from a Euro-centric trading country to an Asia-centric trading company, and Houston is perfectly placed for that.

Many people were surprised, after so many years of having restaurants as tenants, when I opened my own Highland Village restaurant called Up. What they perhaps didn't understand was what you see as a landlord. You have a lot of chain restaurants with good financials, who pay their rent on time and serve the same food here as they serve in Scottsdale. And you have the other extreme: rock-star chef-driven restaurants, many of the chefs living out of town and none of them ever actually cooking. They do draw a lot of breathless praise from food writers, but it's very rare that they last more than two years.

What I'm trying to do at Up is take the best aspects of those chef-driven restaurants and the best aspects of the chains. I get the best ingredients possible, cook them in a very straightforward way and give great value with real food. People go to restaurants, I think, to be social. After all, would you buy half the things you buy if nobody ever saw them? No, make that three-quarters.

DEANEA LeFLORE
Deanea LeFlore serves as chief protocol officer for the City of Houston. As executive director of the Houston Office of Protocol and International Affairs, a division of the Mayor's Office, she has overseen the visits of hundreds of international government officials.

Houston is a world-class international city and Houston's consular corps is a valuable asset. More than ninety nations have chosen Houston as a base from which to officially develop economic, commercial, scientific and cultural relations with this area of the country. Consular officials are also charged with safeguarding the interests of the sending country's citizens traveling through or living in their consular districts. Given the diversity and strength of Houston's economy, international connectivity through our airport system and port, and the rich diversity of our population, many countries find that it makes strategic sense to have representation in Houston. In fact, Houston has the third-largest consular corps in the nation after New York and Los Angeles and the largest in Texas and the southwest United States. Annually our mayor hosts the Consular Forum, which includes a business conference and the Consular Ball, a premiere white-tie event honoring Houston's consular corps and the immeasurable cultural and economic benefits they bring to this region.

Houston has been recognized as the most ethnically diverse metropolitan area in the United States. Our elected officials and the community know the value of international collaboration and the cultural and economic benefits this collaboration brings to our city. For example, Houston has an award-winning international sister cities program. We have seventeen sister city relationships around the globe, each with a dedicated team of volunteer citizen diplomats organizing cultural, education and/or commercial exchange opportunities.

The Houston Office of Protocol and International Affairs, a division of the Mayor's Office, provides assistance to more than 200 international delegations per year headed by visiting ambassadors, cabinet-level ministers, and heads of state and government. On any given day, there is an international government official visiting Houston and often multiple officials. The office serves as the city's liaison to the consular corps and administers Houston's sister city relationships.

The team at the Houston Office of Protocol and International Affairs respects and values the diversity and cultural traditions of our citizens and our international visitors. As a life-long student of languages, international relations and cultural norms, I, and the other members of our team strive to make international delegations feel warmly welcomed in Houston while showing them the many opportunities the city has to offer. For instance, in a single weekend I had the opportunity to give welcome remarks in Spanish and present certificates of appreciation to visiting poets from Latin America, enjoyed a concert hosted by Sister Cities of Houston, took Arabic lessons at the Arab American Culture and Community Center and attended Mexico's Independence Day celebration at Miller Outdoor Theater, along with thousands of other Houstonians. These are just a few examples of Houston's diversity and the opportunities available to our residents.

This level of diversity is both supported and enhanced by an airport system that connects Houston on a global scale. International travel at Bush Airport has increased by more than 60 percent over the past decade, while Hobby Airport is preparing to re-introduce international air travel to its passengers in 2015, by offering regional service to Latin America and the Caribbean.

The city's key role in space exploration history was forever cemented in 1969, when "Houston" became the first word ever spoken from the surface of the moon. Other historic moments include Houston's hosting of the G-7 Summit in 1990 (The forum brought together in Houston the heads of government of Canada, France, Italy, Japan, United Kingdom, the United States, West Germany and the president of the European Commission) and Deng Xiaoping's famous visit to Houston in 1979.

Once you arrive here it doesn't matter from where you came—1 in 5 Houstonians were born in another country; I strongly believe that talent, hard work and commitment are rewarded here. I consider myself fortunate to have been able to leverage the opportunities a diverse city provides for gaining cross-cultural understanding to become more effective in supporting our city's international development objectives as well as for personal enrichment. Being able to organize or take part in cultural or religious events, official ceremonies, as well as international business events and trade missions has provided me with a deeper knowledge and understanding of how to forge and sustain mutually beneficial international relationships.

CHASE UNTERMEYER

International business consultant Chase Untermeyer served for three years as United States Ambassador to Qatar on appointment of President George W. Bush. He has held both elected and appointed office at all four levels of government—local, state, national, and international—for more than 35 years, with work in journalism, academia and business as well.

Perhaps because Houston was created out of nothing more than the confluence of two bayous, our city has always welcomed anyone and everyone willing to work hard to build the community. And if they did all right for themselves along the way, so much the better.

I received a personal lesson from this phenomenon when I was fortunate enough to sit next to the late Nina Cullinan at a function held about 1980. She was the daughter of Joseph Cullinan, the founder of Texaco, who came to Houston right after Spindletop. Miss Cullinan became a major patron of the arts in Houston, particularly of the Museum of Fine Arts. I asked if she minded the fact that newcomers in Houston, by generous outlays of cash to organizations like the Museum, could land literally beside her on prestige boards. Miss Cullinan's response was swift. "Oh no," she said. "When we came here, we had no letters of introduction to people, and yet we were welcomed."

The pioneering television journalist Ray Miller liked to speak of the debt Houston owes to "bachelor millionaires" like George Hermann and M.D. Anderson, plus the childless widower William Marsh Rice. One might add to this list the names of bachelorette millionaire ladies like Miss Cullinan and Ima Hogg. Lacking descendants, they made us all beneficiaries in their wills.

Of course, towering over all our city's history was Jesse Holman Jones, who literally built Houston, saved its banks during the Great Depression, and then went to Washington as head of the Reconstruction Finance Corporation and as Secretary of Commerce. He was among those who gathered for liquid companionship in Suite 8F of the old Lamar Hotel, a group that included George and Herman Brown, Gus Wortham, Leopold Meyer and Governor Will and Oveta Culp Hobby. While this was indeed a very elite group, they key thing is that they, like those who came before and after them, recognized that Houston would grow greater only if the base of power was constantly widened. This was a startling conclusion, since history teaches that such people typically hoard all power unto themselves. As a result of such forward-looking people, Houston has the healthiest racial and ethnic climate of any big city in the United States.

This is a blessing of such magnitude that we often take it for granted. But it is one that we cannot forget and cannot fail to remind younger generations. More than that, we must certainly do our part to live up to the honored Houston tradition of public and civic service ourselves and to extend it to as many others as we can. Sixty years ago, Lon Tinkle, the literary editor of *The Dallas Morning News*, wrote: "It is hard not to feel affection for a city victimized by a magnificent obsession. Houston is obsessed by the future. Houstonians co-exist in the present and the future. What they don't have now, they will have next week. Tomorrow is right at home on Houston's doorstep."

LARRY PAYNE

Larry Payne is a consultant to corporations large and small, helping them embrace the concept of "servant leadership." He is the author of The Heart of HoUSton: Lessons in Servant Leadership *and the host of weekly interview programs on Houston radio and television. He has also worked in various capacities at City Hall during four different administrations.*

As the 4th largest city in America, Houston is multi-cultural, multi-ethnic, multi-lingual, multi-religious and multi-everything else. Yet while it might fly in the face of what some people think, Houston's business community has been quick to embrace the idea of "servant leadership," whether they call it that or something else. This truth for me has always been something I've been able to enjoy in this city: working with a broad-based collection of human beings, that reservoir and resource of people who all see things, though sometimes differently, in a big picture way.

I work with corporations and not-for-profit organizations to give them a way of life, one that in the beginning improves how they feel about each other and in the end improves their bottom line. Servant leadership, the way I try to share it, impacts every aspect and sphere of life, from society to politics, education to healthcare. We are put on the face of this earth for one reason only: to help serve other human beings. When people see how you live your life, being a servant to others, you become a leader. It's the difference between telling somebody "I love you" and actually showing them.

I grew up in racially segregated Orange, Texas, in the age of the Ku Klux Klan. I was called or heard the n-word every day, and I had to fight somebody most days, since in that world if you fought somebody and beat him, you were better than he was. Now I understand that we have to see ourselves as connected to each other. Once you see that you have to have other human beings in order to be successful, you start building relationships built on mutual trust and respect. Those are not things you throw together in the heat of battle, when the times are tough. You have to develop relationships with people you need *before* you need them. That's what we're striving for here in Houston. We don't have a choice but to get it right.

The biggest challenge we face here is fixing our public urban education system. We have to figure out how to produce not a good but an excellent system that serves every student's needs. Essentially, the regular urban public schools in Houston—not counting charter schools and things like that—are segregated again. Last time I checked, among more than 210,000 students in HISD classrooms, only 8.7% were Anglo. For us to have the future workforce we all need and want, we have to change this. If you're not educated, you're not able to take your rightful place and compete. You really don't have a future.

I would characterize Houston as having an open and caring business community that's always looking for creative ideas and solutions, not only to business problems but also to community problems. If you bring something to the table here, and if you're able to articulate it, we'll help you accomplish your goal. It's a matter of seeing not individuals or persons but fellow human beings. You do that and you'll treat people the way you want to be treated. It's simple, really.

DAVID DEWHURST

A native Texan, military veteran, businessman and rancher, David Dewhurst has served as Lieutenant Governor and President of the Texas Senate since 2003. During his time in office, Texas has had six consecutive balanced budgets and leads the country in job creation, making Texas the number one place to start a business and raise a family. Outside of politics, David Dewhurst lives in Houston with his wife, Tricia, and their young daughter, Carolyn.

Every time I fly into Houston, I actually feel a heartbeat, a contagious energy that pulsates in Houston, which I really don't sense in other cities around the country. Houston is not only my hometown, but it has helped make me who and what I am today. Not only is it the largest city in Texas, it's a microcosm of what is truly great about Texas. With a diverse economy and population, it is chock-full of the kind of opportunity for which our state is known.

Everything about Houston and its people is unique. Our Houston Medical Center and world-class hospitals, our international energy industry (a sector I'm involved in), our emerging high-tech industry and our universities are second to none. Houston is so large that we have three professional sports teams—Astros, Texans, and Rockets. At the same time, you can enjoy the beaches of Galveston and the Gulf of Mexico and the excitement of NASA in the same drive. Not that far outside Houston, we even have pastures full of horses, and one of my personal favorites is the Houston Rodeo, where I have volunteered time, supported, and even competed regularly in NCHA Cutting competitions. Houstonians are proud to be from Houston, and it shows.

As Lieutenant Governor of Texas, I work hard every day to make sure that Texas is a safe, prosperous place to live. I've worked to help create the best business climate in the country, and today Texas is number one in virtually every economic and financial category worth reporting. And prosperity means opportunities for everyone. The impact of that extends to Houston, where I have pushed (with success) for more economic development, a bigger investment in public safety and improvements to the quality of public education. People keep voting for Houston and Texas with their feet, so we're all doing something right together.

I grew up in Houston with two younger brothers, the sons of a single mother who worked as a secretary to feed and clothe my brothers and me after my dad was killed by a drunk driver. My mother and my church taught me my Christian faith, integrity and hard work. The lessons I learned in church, in the public school classroom, on the basketball court at Lamar High School and working at the Port of Houston during high school have all helped shape my success as a public servant.

When it comes to defining Houston, there are almost too many moments of greatness to pick just one. However, the way Houston welcomed the refugees from Hurricane Katrina showed the world how Texans care for their neighbors. Watching state leaders working alongside city leaders working alongside community leaders and pastors to welcome people who arrived with nothing to their name was a remarkable showing of the real Texas and Houston heart. The oil bust of the early 1980s was another defining moment for Houston. In the aftermath of that bust, Houstonians picked themselves up by their bootstraps. Houston both revived itself and emerged as a more robust, diversified and stronger economy.

While Houston is my home, I'm in Dallas frequently. Dallas is a fantastic city, sophisticated, bustling with energy and growing businesses. It has a great quality of life and is the home of many dear friends of ours. Whether the Texans and the Cowboys are competing on the football field, or the Chambers of Commerce are competing to lure even more jobs to Texas from across the country and around the world, any rivalry between Houston and Dallas brings out the best in both cities and makes our whole state better.

TONY SANCHEZ

Tony Sanchez Jr. is chairman of the board and CEO of Sanchez Oil & Gas Corporation, a family-owned company engaged in exploration and development of oil and natural gas. Mr. Sanchez earned both his B.A. and Doctor of Jurisprudence (J.D.) from St. Mary's University in San Antonio, Texas. Mr. Sanchez and his wife have four children, six grandchildren, and are actively involved in community, educational and health care initiatives.

It is refreshing to see, and I take pride in the fact, that Houston has become one of the most racially/ethnically diverse metropolitan areas in the nation. This diversity has vast influences throughout the city with many unique events held which celebrate the varied culture of Houstonians.

Statistics have shown alarming high school dropout rates for Latinos and African-Americans, especially from economically-challenged families. My family and I have joined forces with a unique, innovative, educational model offered by the Catholic Church and the Jesuits that tackles these very issues, not only for the students in need, but for the future of our city and inevitably of our state and country. The school is Cristo Rey Jesuit Preparatory High School. The students are required to take part in the school's Corporate Work-Study Program, whereby they earn nearly 50% of their private-school education working one day a week in blue-ribbon corporations across Houston. The students build invaluable corporate skills while working alongside seasoned professionals.

A company such as ours could not thrive as successfully as it has and reach the same levels of prosperity in any other city. As much as I love Laredo, Houston is the headquarters of Sanchez Oil & Gas. With Houston being what everyone considers the "hub" of the oil and gas industry, the access to related technology, knowledgeable workforce and geographic location provides the perfect combination for success.

In mid-2007 the U.S. fell into one of the worst recessions since the Great Depression. Fortunately, Texas cities were essentially unscathed when compared to their counterparts in other parts of the country. Most impressively, amongst the ten largest metropolitan areas; Houston was the first major city which was able to recover all the jobs that were lost during the economic downturn. As of March 2013, Houston is recorded as not only regaining all the lost jobs but has since added more than two jobs for every one lost due to the crash. Houston gained 230.5% of the jobs back, with Dallas coming in second with 164.2% (U.S. Bureau of Labor Statistics). To date, Houston's unemployment rate is well below the national average.

Houston most definitely embodies an "aspirational" city. In 10 years (2000-2010) the Houston metropolitan area added over 1.2 million people and continues to grow, securing its position as the 4th largest city in the country. This represents more population growth than any other metropolitan area in the United States. Much of the migration stems from the multiple strong industries present in Houston including healthcare, energy and aerospace, as well as being a major port city.

Houston was shown to be a city inhabited by people with a great sense of empathy, concern and kindness in 2005 when as many as 250,000 Louisiana residents had been left displaced by Hurricane Katrina and they were welcomed into our city for refuge. Not only is Houston diverse but so is the terrain and geography. Within a short drive time you can access beaches, rolling hills, bayous, lakes and rivers. You can experience city, suburban and country/rural living. There is something for everyone.

TRAMMELL S. CROW

The founder of Earth Day in Dallas, Trammell S. Crow grew up as heir to the Trammell Crow real estate fortune in Turtle Creek. He was first introduced to environmentalism by his brother in the sixth grade and, coming to believe that business and industry can play significant roles in green improvements, now oversees one the nation's largest Earth Day events.

As a lifelong resident of Dallas—having lived elsewhere only for college, a year or two in Denver and a year or two in Houston—I have always been an ardent admirer of my hometown, a walking Chamber of Commerce and an ardent tour guide. My pride stems from good fortune, family business and experiencing all phases of life here. In other words, Dallas has been good to me.

Parkland Hospital comes to mind as a symbol of our family's contribution to Dallas. The resuscitation of this landmark on the corner of Oaklawn and Maple avenues will cause both streets and the entire

DALLAS: *Bank of America Plaza*

surrounding area to improve. Our family has always been committed to working hard, having a positive attitude and acting on a sense of self-reliance and achievement. In that sense, we are like our city, which is made up of positivists, optimists, people who believe in the American Dream. This city and state tend to allow free enterprise.

Dallas has a lot of special attributes. Some of the ones that matter most to me are fashion, the wholesale and retail trade, too much materialism, Neiman-Marcus, the Dallas Market Center, DFW Airport, Texas Instruments and its resulting high-tech sector, a tragic segregation of ethnic and economic groups, strong religious commitments, vibrant restaurants and entertainment, friendliness and simple philosophies. In Dallas, we are all about hard work, hard play, socializing, sports and family.

For its part, Houston has always been a kindred spirit to me, with friends, competitive and complimentary business, and freewheeling gung-ho business and other aspirations. I've always been slightly envious of its oil and gas industries, its port and its international population.

DAVID MARTINEAU

Now exploration manager for Pitts Oil Company, David received a Bachelor of Science degree in geology from The University of Texas at Austin and is chairman of TIPRO, which has fought on both state and federal levels to preserve the ability for independents to explore and produce oil and natural gas.

Even though I've been working in oil and gas here since 1969, Dallas is not really an oil and gas kind of town. It's an insurance town for sure, and it's got every bank you've ever heard of. When it comes to oil and gas, that's mostly a Houston thing. Based on some of the political battles we're fighting here right now, it looks like it might stay that way. Years ago, the city collected $34.8 million in bonus money from companies leasing land within the city limits for drilling, and when the recession hit in 2008, of course the city went and spent that money right away. Now that the companies who paid that money are applying for permits to actually drill, the city is turning them down. In terms of distance from the lease line these days, it just can't be done.

Right now there is no oil production within the city limits of Dallas. Compare this to Fort Worth, which does allow drilling. There are 1,700 wells in Fort Worth, and it's been a tremendous economic boon. I'm afraid that in Dallas we're listening to a lot of environmentalists who sometimes just aren't telling the truth, but the politicians are afraid to do what's right for the good of the city. They have these movies that came out, and they show those to the City Council. If people have a problem, for years sometimes, if they can possibly blame it on the oil companies, they will. I was just downtown listening to the battle going on. Let me tell you: the city doesn't make these kinds of rules for anybody who wants to come in here and build a hotel.

I'm sure one of the main reasons Dallas has grown over the years is our location. We have a busy airport and we're right in the middle of everything, about the same distance by air from the East Coast and the West Coast. Years ago, FedEx even came to Dallas with the idea of locating its headquarters here, for exactly that reason. Then, when they didn't get the tax break they wanted, they decided to locate in Memphis instead.

Today our mayor is very active in trying to make Dallas grow—but we definitely have a north Dallas and a south Dallas, with most on the economy concentrated in the north. Downtown we've got more museums and concert halls than ever before, most of them built recently. And there are lots of different things happening to draw smaller companies into relocating here, even when the big companies have chosen to be farther out in north Dallas to be near the airport or where employees with young families want to live.

There's more downtown development on the way, too. The work ethic is great in Dallas. And you can go to the basketball game or to the opera. That's what young people want, so lots of companies are moving here. The city recently converted five acres on top of the Woodall Rodgers Freeway into the Klyde Warren Park. Just the other night there were 3,000 people sitting in that park watching opera on video screens.

D'ANN PETERSON

D'Ann Petersen is a consulting business economist, formerly a long time member of the Federal Reserve Bank of Dallas' regional group, where she conducted research on regional economic issues and produced articles for various bank publications. Petersen tracks the real estate and construction sectors and spent numerous years contributing to the Federal Reserve's survey of regional economic conditions.

Since the Great Recession of 2008, Dallas and to some degree the rest of Texas, has turned around faster than most other parts of the country. The job growth here is strong, attracting many people to Dallas from other states. Every single highway seems to be under construction, which isn't fun for those of us who live here, but it says something about the way the city is growing. The local housing market has seen an increase in demand and prices, but we're still much more affordable than most other large cities. We have a vibrant urban core now, which wasn't always the case, and that's attracting a lot of young people who like to walk to work in the morning and walk to restaurants and other entertainment at night. Dallas is much more of an urban city than it was even 10 years ago.

Innovation plays a large role in attracting firms and people to Dallas Fort Worth. While the first microchip was invented at Texas Instruments in the 1950s, in the 1990s the region matured into a high tech center. The ties to defense electronics and energy have been catalysts for not only high tech growth, but growth in professional services, including accounting, legal, engineering and consulting. Recently, job growth has been strong in these sectors as well as in the financial sector, in part due to growth in insurance jobs created in response to health care reform. The Metroplex's universities, defense and high tech firms have attracted scientists as well as engineers, skilled electricians and telecom workers.

As for individual industries, finance is doing quite well—it's always been part of our culture here—and insurance, especially with the Affordable Care Act. We went through a high tech bust and lost some of our prowess there. Dallas led the state in the number of tech workers, even though people tended to think of Austin first. We're strong in business and legal services. And we're lucky to be located in the middle of Texas and somewhat in the middle of America, because that's let us be a distribution and logistics hub. We are close to our most important trading partner, Mexico. We had a large share of energy companies here in the 1980s, but many of those companies ended up moving to Houston. So that's definitely a difference between the two cities.

The housing market and the apartment market are both thriving. The S&P Case-Shiller Home Price Index showed Dallas-Fort Worth home prices rising at almost the same pace as the nation this year. According to the index, Dallas-Fort Worth home prices rose above the 2007 peak in April of 2013. U.S. prices are rising at a fast pace but remain below their pre-recession peak. Single-family existing home inventories in Dallas are near record lows, well below the six-month supply marker, suggesting a tight market and rising prices.

Among the challenges we're facing, the infrastructure here needs to catch up with the economic growth. We have a bus and train system, but I think we need to do better in that department. Generally we have an educated workforce, with our local universities doing a good job, but our Dallas school system needs improving, and leaders are working towards strides to educate our young people better. There's been a lot of talk and concern lately about our water usage, which has become a big issue for many large, fast-growing American cities. We need more sources of water because if our supply gets low, it's going to cost us a lot to look elsewhere for our water needs.

There's plenty of reason for hope, though. Dallas simply is a great place to be. We have a very committed business community. The dynamics of our economy, primarily transportation and trade, along with the professional service-oriented economy, are going to keep expanding and drawing people. I believe that our urban core and the suburbs feel closer, more together now than they have in the past, and that's not just because I work downtown. Like many people, I live in the suburbs, but my family visits downtown and uptown regularly—especially because of the new parks and gardens, along with events in the Arts District.

GINGER REEDER

Ginger Reeder is vice president for corporate communications of the Neiman Marcus Group, which includes the namesake luxury department store as well as Bergdorf Goodman and several upscale catalog retailers, including Horchow. Founded in 1907, Neiman Marcus retains its corporate headquarters in Dallas, with other Texas stores located in Houston, Austin and San Antonio.

Lots of people in Dallas have shopped at Neiman Marcus for generations, and people who've lived in this city for a very long time feel a special kind of possessiveness about our brand. Yet we have forty-one stores in many different states. And really, I'm not sure if the people in Houston who've been shopping at our Galleria store since it opened in the 1970s don't think of Neiman Marcus as a beloved *Houston* store. It's a kind of Texas pride now, one that transcends Dallas or Houston, or even San Antonio or Austin.

In his book *Minding the Store*, I think Stanley Marcus said it best—the success of Neiman Marcus was more about the personalities of the founders than about the personality of Dallas. All three founders were from Dallas, of course, and all three had worked in retail in Dallas. And there were plenty of reasons a store like this might not work, as people told them again and again. There were more saloons than doctors in Dallas in 1907, and there weren't too many paved streets. People said that opening a retail store with a special emphasis on luxury wasn't a very good idea. But the three wanted to come home and do something with some money they'd made in Georgia. And what they wanted to do became known as Neiman Marcus. It was the store they'd always dreamed of and talked about when they were bored working retail. Clearly, the entrepreneurial spirit was alive and well in Dallas in 1907.

It was in the 1950s, when Stanley Marcus took over from his father, that big things really started happening. Marketing was his gift--his genius–as he demonstrated with Neiman Marcus Fortnight at the flagship store. People didn't have the Travel Channel to watch back then, and there was no easy way to get to Europe. Turning the store into a different country every year was something phenomenal. I grew up in Shreveport, Louisiana, and my mother drove us over to see Neiman Marcus during the holidays every year. The Fortnight promotion ended in the late 1970s. By then, they had run out of countries and had even made up a country one year.

People all over the world are buying online from Neiman Marcus now, and we ship to more than a hundred countries. So we don't really think of ourselves as a Dallas store. Still, our headquarters are here and our buying is done here, instead of New York. We like to think of ourselves as a good hometown child, even if the main growth of our company has come outside Dallas and outside Texas.

The Neiman Marcus Christmas Book started out as a simple holiday card to remind people to come in and shop. We had His and Her gifts by the early 1950s, but it wasn't until 1959 that the Christmas Book started attracting national attention. Edward R. Murrow of CBS News would call Stanley Marcus and ask him what those crazy Texans were buying for Christmas, and that's how he knew he had to have a story on hand by coming up with gifts chosen more for publicity than for salability. The first year it was a Texas steer, either on the hoof or as steaks, plus a man dressed in black tie with a silver serving-cart. This publicity was the key to our being able to move outside Texas. People had heard or read about His and Her camels, and there was something romantic about being able to buy lipstick from the same store where you could buy camels.

ERROL McKOY

Errol McKoy started working for Six Flags Over Texas in 1961 while still in college. After graduation he was selected by the Six Flags Corporation to run the Lake Amusement Area of the New York World's Fair, then transferred to Atlanta to head up human resources of the new Six Flags theme park, rising to general manager in 1969 at the age of twenty-six. Over the next 23 years he also managed Six Flags Over Texas and served as executive vice president of Six Flags Corporation. He joined the State Fair of Texas as president in 1988.

Dallas is larger than life, and its citizens live life big. As far back as 1934, civic leaders have been willing to tackle big projects. In 1934, largely through the efforts of civic leader R.L. Thornton, Fair Park was selected as the central exposition site for the proposed Texas Centennial celebration. Construction began on a $25 million project that transformed the existing fairgrounds into a masterpiece of art and imagination. The 1936 Texas Centennial Exposition attracted more than six million people during its six-month run.

The city of Dallas has been the home of the State Fair of Texas since 1886. Dallas is the perfect setting for the largest State Fair in the nation and offers visitors a unique opportunity to experience the arts and enjoy great food and a variety of sporting events. I had the distinction of being the president of the State Fair of Texas when the Fair became the Fried Food Capital of Texas. We developed an annual competition known as the Big Tex® Choice Awards. The annual event has brought the event worldwide attention.

The citizens of Dallas have welcomed change and growth at the State Fair of Texas. The Fair has worked with the city of Dallas to continue to improve the historic Cotton Bowl Stadium and attract more games and events. Dallasites continue to flock to the Fair each year in ever-increasing numbers. The Fair is currently planning future annual events that will draw more visitors to the park on a year-round basis.

After the assassination of President Kennedy, Dallas refused to let the event define the city. The city has advanced in the arts, sports, education and entertainment. Today, Dallas and its leaders aspire to develop the downtown area and draw more people into the area to live and raise families. Dallas perseveres, rises to meet challenges, and embraces change. Dallas is a great city to call "home" and provides the perfect setting to raise a family, own a business and become involved in the community. Texas is big enough to have more than one great city—and it is lucky for Houston that's the case.

MICHAEL M. BOONE

A resident of Dallas since he was five, Mike Boone holds both an accounting degree and a law degree from SMU. He is a co-founder of the law firm Haynes and Boone where he specializes in corporate law and mergers and acquisitions. During the past 40-plus years, he has been very involved in Dallas civic affairs including having served as chairman of the Dallas Citizens Council, president of the Highland Park School Board and a member of the SMU Board of Trustees. At the state level, he has been heavily involved in Texas public school finance and higher education issues.

If you ask the people who've moved their corporate headquarters to Dallas over the past thirty years, they'll tell you that Dallas is exceptionally friendly and accepting and, moreover, it's a city where people want to succeed—and where they want you to succeed as well. Dallasites have always strived to make their city a better place in which to live, to do business and to raise a family. So, whenever I think of Dallas' many achievements, I think immediately of how much this city loves to compete to be the best. This competitive spirit has driven Dallas's emergence as a strong global city.

Dallas is the largest metropolitan area in the nation not located on a navigable body of water. When it was founded in the early 1800s, it was just a place located on the open prairie lands of North Texas. There was simply no natural geographic reason why it would one day become a major global city. However, during the intervening years, thanks to the vision and resolve of its civic leaders and the spirit of its people, Dallas willed itself into greatness.

Two transformative events changed the course of Dallas' future. First, in the late 1800s, the city seized upon a strategic growth opportunity by successfully competing to become the location of the intersection of the north-south and east-west railroad lines in North Texas. As a result, Dallas grew into a thriving distribution center and from that into a major center for banking and commerce. The second transformative event was the building of the DFW airport in the early 1970s. Today, it is the 4th busiest airport in the world and the major catalyst for Dallas's growth via the strength of its global impact. It has become the major market differentiator in Dallas's success, on a global basis, in the competition for corporate headquarter relocations, new business startups and talented people.

Dallas would not be where it is today if it were not for the local business leaders who have, throughout its history, personally stepped up to give of their time, brain power and financial resources to help our city be successful. That is why the greatest challenge facing Dallas may well be its ability to continue to secure business leaders who will likewise engage in leading the city forward. In a similar vein, with the changing demographics of Texas, our city must strive to develop strong Hispanic and African-American civic leaders. Having a strong and diverse core of civic leaders really matters to Dallas' future.

New York, California and a handful of other states have each, at different points in time, been viewed as being "king of the mountain" among the states by reason of their economic strength, business climate, global presence, cultural amenities and other factors. Today, the State of Texas can lay claim to that position. But what about tomorrow? Will Texas fall from this lofty position as its predecessors have? Will we avoid the missteps of our competitors? The answer to these questions will depend in large part on whether Texas—and especially its two leading cities, Dallas and Houston—continue to be relentless in their efforts to be better. After all, there is no finish line in this race to claim "bragging rights" for being the best.

KAY BAILEY HUTCHISON

Kay Bailey Hutchison is a former U.S. Senator from Texas. She was named one of the 30 most powerful women in America by Ladies Home Journal *in 2001 and one of the 100 most powerful women in the world by* Forbes *magazine in 2005. The first woman to represent Texas in the U.S. Senate, Hutchison also became the first Texas U.S. Senator to receive more than four million votes in a single election.*

Texas' entrepreneurial spirit is evident in both Dallas and Houston and it sets them apart from the large cities in other states that would be in their peer group. They are friendly, they welcome newcomers and they encourage businesses that add to a vibrant economy. In

Houston, the early base was oil-related, including refineries; diversification includes shipping and medical services. In Dallas, the early base was banking; diversification includes technology, aviation and energy.

In my Senate career, I worked with cities to achieve their highest priorities; not their wish list, but their need list. Priorities requested for Houston included dredging the Ship Channel and Turning Basin to accommodate the largest ships; working with the Department of Defense to transfer the reserve base at Old Spanish Trail to Ellington Field. This opened the base land for MD Anderson to purchase for expansion and preserved the Ellington asset as a reserve base rather than its destined closure. I worked to assure Houston's METRO rail project would be fully funded and also to assure human space exploration would remain a priority for NASA—for the American economy and to continue the valuable Johnson Space Center jobs and assets.

The priorities requested for Dallas included carrying the legislation to phase out the Wright Amendment to open Love Field as a limited inner city airport without geographic restrictions; assuring DART continued full funding; and helping the City of Dallas achieve flood protection from the Trinity River while developing it as a transportation and recreational asset. Both Dallas and Houston have major academic research institutions, and I worked to assure they had access to federal priorities for research.

From this you can determine two things: Both Dallas and Houston now prioritize mass transit after years of investing heavily in highways, but they still are working to overcome gridlock. The economic contribution of academic and medical universities is significant in both, and each is a center of excellence with national recognition.

Both Dallas and Houston are investing in beautification, economic diversification and higher educational institutions (both quality universities and medical schools that will attract research that enhances economic development). Both have increased the amount of major donations for arts and culture. Both cities have entrepreneurial business leaders, arts and culture, quality real estate development that prioritize conservation, green spaces and beautification.

As for lifestyle, both have that special Texas blend of laid back and sophistication.

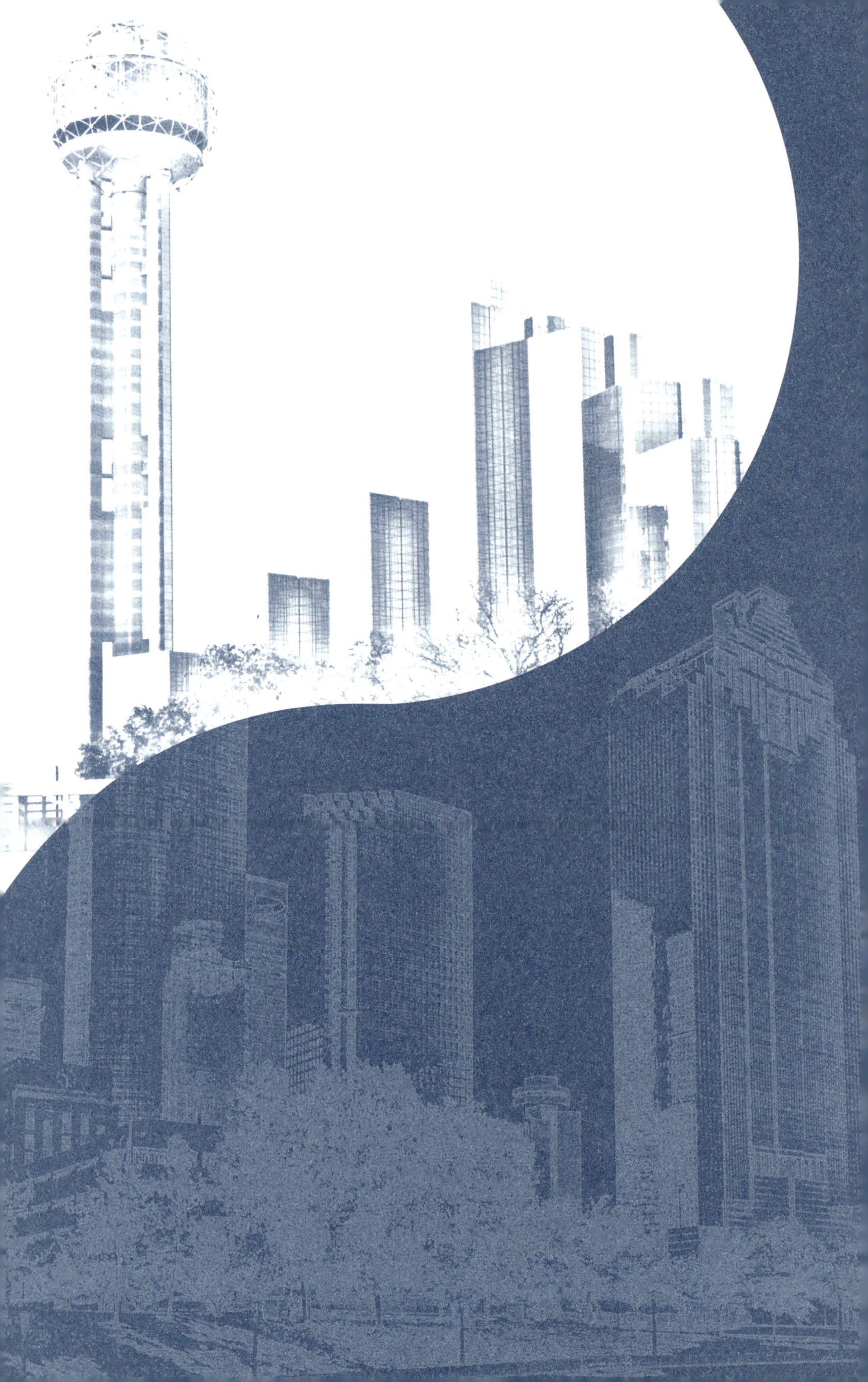

02

SOCIETY & PHILANTHROPY

Getting rich is part of the Texas mystique, and it's hard to locate too many people on the face of this earth who haven't heard of J.R. Ewing and others of questionable ethics who've played the high-risk "feast or famine" system to untold wealth. But when we look deeper into the state's history by way of its wealthiest, we paint a portrait mostly removed from J.R., as beloved a Texas icon as he was and is. Fact is, many of the most affluent citizens in Dallas and Houston are also among the most generous.

In general, philanthropy is a traditional family commitment—meaning that multi-generational wealth that has for decades accepted a responsibility for community service continues to be that way. Many of the youngest philanthropists credit their parents for teaching them how and why; some even credit their grandparents. Some family commitments go back to the generation that first acquired the wealth, which is impressive considering the scraping and scrapping that are so often required. The social teachings of religion, primarily Christianity and Judaism, are regularly cited as reasons to share the bounty that God has given.

Despite the traditionalism deep in the heart of Texas philanthropy, it is certainly changing, both in style and in substance. Two main strands of philanthropy continue to be evident: the arts-and-culture strand and the help-the-less-fortunate strand. And the leadership of Houston and Dallas will tell you both are important. Arts and culture—opera, ballet, symphony, theater and museums—are, even beyond local boosterism, essential to creating a world-class city that attracts and keeps major corporations. And for those philanthropists drawn to the less glamorous worlds of housing the homeless, feeding the hungry or rescuing the abused, both cities offer ample opportunities to do so. In addition, Houston and Dallas both have long and strong traditions of philanthropy relating to medicine, with Houston's Medical Center the largest but by no means the only example.

Today, younger philanthropists are continuing to support all these types of work for the good of their communities, while also digging deeper into the most baffling of current issues. Some are funding, for instance, detailed and series studies of childhood obesity and prison reform, with an eye toward doing what the best philanthropy always aspires to do—make a difference.

RUTH ALTSHULER

In 2013, as a capstone to a long lifetime of good works, Dallas philanthropist Ruth Altshuler was asked to chair the commemoration of the 50th anniversary of President John F. Kennedy's assassination. Her father, Carr P. Collins, founded Fidelity Union Life Insurance Co. in Dallas in 1927, which eventually became one of the largest insurance firms in America.

I certainly remember the day John F. Kennedy was shot, and all I heard people saying back then was that Dallas was a "city of hate." That just wears me out. If there was any hate going on here, I certainly didn't know about it. That's really what we hoped to say to the world when the mayor asked me to chair the fiftieth anniversary: that as cities go, Dallas is about as good as you can get. I love this city. I was born here, and I'm proud of all the things we've accomplished. If anybody ever did a survey in this country, measuring philanthropic giving and volunteer work, I think Dallas would have to be number one.

I've been doing this for 65 years, and I've never seen any other

DALLAS: *Northwood Country Club*

city giving or working like Dallas does. Our Junior League is supposed to be the biggest and most effective in the world. You know, Albert Schweitzer always talked about the power of example, as opposed to everything else that's just a lot of talk. My father was a poor boy in Beaumont. He sold apples on the train and newspapers on the corner. Eventually he started an insurance company that was very successful, but there were many years when my parents did without.

One time the pastor of our First Baptist Church called my father and mother and other couples together and asked them to make a major donation. My father told the pastor he'd donate $5000, which was probably like $500,000 today. My mother cried all the way home on the streetcar and just kept asking him, "How are we going to donate $5000 when we don't have a dime." My father told her, "I'm walking into the bank tomorrow and borrowing the money." I may have grown up well-to-do, but I also grew up with that example.

I joined our Junior League as a twenty-five-year-old bride, and they took me on a tour of a Dallas I'd never seen. We went to Parkland Hospital and the Lighthouse for the Blind and Goodwill Industries. I was just so overwhelmed. There was so much need and so much that needed to be done. That was the turning point in my life.

When the mayor turned to me to chair the Kennedy commemoration, he said he wanted something very dignified, very appropriate. It's not a celebration; it's a commemoration. And since I've been friends with David McCullough for years, I asked him to come read something. What he ended up choosing to read were not his words at all but President Kennedy's. As much as I love David's writing, I think that was the right choice. We knew we wanted something serious and somber. We wanted to appreciate a life.

If someone who'd just moved here came to me and said she wanted my advice, I'd start by asking her what she was interested in. Doing volunteer work in Dallas is a great way to meet people and get involved. Before you know it, you're going to dinner at people's houses, and then you're hosting dinners of your own. My heart has always been in feeding the poor, but others are more committed to the arts or to our fine universities. It takes all kinds, of course. There's so much you can do in Dallas.

LINDA PERRYMAN EVANS

Prior to becoming president and CEO of the Dallas-based Meadows Foundation, Linda Perryman Evans was an active partner in the public relations firm of Stern, Nathan & Perryman. Previously she served as executive director of the Dallas Welcoming Committee, the city's non-partisan host committee for the 1984 Republican National Convention. A graduate of The University of Texas at Austin, Linda worked in Washington from 1976 through 1983.

I think many of us in Dallas have watched our parents volunteer and contribute their resources. As a very young girl I learned to wrap small presents that my mother would take to the elderly who lived in homes and who otherwise wouldn't have anything for Christmas. My parents' generation instilled in us the importance of giving back to our community. In many ways, that's what sets America apart, our nation's generosity to those who are less fortunate. But I have to say: I spent several years in Washington and they don't have anything close to what Dallas does.

Our city has been built by of the generosity of individuals and foundations. There's a culture here that we can do anything we set our minds to if we work together. We are surrounded in Dallas by incredibly giving people. It's the way our museums have been built, the way our performing arts center has been built and the way our charitable organizations have thrived. If you are a young person who starts your career in Dallas, you simply find your way to that giving-back spirit. When I was starting out, I had several wonderful mentors in philanthropy. It's those city leaders whom many of us have watched and learned from. My great uncle Al Meadows left all his wealth to The Meadows Foundation, so that we could direct its use in perpetuity and find the joy in giving that he always found.

That's how it always was for people and companies that were started here, that became successful here. They were typically led by people who felt immense gratitude to Dallas for being the place they generated their wealth. These people were the foundation of most of what you see in Dallas today. In recent years, more companies have moved here from elsewhere, so they don't necessarily have the deep roots or the same values that our oldest families and businesses have. I've been pleased, though, that in several high-profile projects like our performing arts center, companies that moved to Dallas have become leaders both in financial contributions and in offering their talents to manage the money better.

Over the years, our foundation has decided to focus on three broad areas: mental health, the environment and public education. Mental health, in particular, has grown in importance, especially in many rural Texas communities that don't have any kind of healthcare available. One in four people in this country have or have had some form of mental illness. We know that if we treat people upfront, it's much less expensive. With the proper treatment, these people can lead long, happy and productive lives. We're working to bring this issue out of the darkness and into the light.

We are also taking a leadership role in advising and encouraging family foundations as a method of giving with many key advantages. One of the greatest qualities of America is the ability to generate wealth and the freedom to give it to organizations and causes that you feel passionate about. The idea of families working together toward this goal is very important, because it passes the philanthropic spirit from one generation to the next. I have cousins in eleven states and in Canada, and my generation is very close because we've all worked together to develop ways of giving. It's an incredible gift to our family.

ALBERT L. REYES

Dr. Albert L. Reyes is the sixth president and CEO in the 135-year history of Buckner International, a global Christian ministry that seeks justice for "the least of these" by providing care and resources for orphans and at-risk children in the United States and more than 50 other countries. Buckner International also advises national governments on children's issues and legislation to ensure lasting changes for at-risk children.

The thing I am most proud of about Dallas is our history of serving disadvantaged people and helping those in need. Beyond our city's reputation as a business center, we also have a history dating back to

1879 of benevolent work among vulnerable children, orphans and the elderly. Buckner International is one of the oldest continuous operating enterprises in the history of Dallas. The founder, Robert Cooke Buckner, established the first orphanage west of the Mississippi right here in Dallas just after the Civil War. The John Neely Bryan Cabin was built as the first homestead on the banks of the Trinity in 1841. This same cabin ended up on the Pinson Land, a few miles east of downtown Dallas on land purchased by Robert Cooke Buckner to house the Buckner Children's Home in 1879.

My first job after college was here in downtown Dallas in the Magnolia Building where the Flying Pegasus sits. I worked for US Telephone in the 1980s during the post-deregulation era of the Bell Telephone system. It was an exciting time to enter the work force. The company became US Sprint, GTE Sprint, and later, Sprint. I worked for Sprint for seven years while I was in graduate school at Southwestern Seminary in Fort Worth.

To me, the city's defining moment was the day we chose Dallas as our name. Prior to this it was named Pete's Corner. We were named after the 11th vice president of the United States, George Mifflin Dallas. He ran for office on a platform that featured the annexation of Texas into the Union. Today, I think we have the opportunity to lead the nation with a dual identity of dynamic commerce and compassionate service to our citizens. These might be inextricably linked. Dallas is enterprising, innovative, creative, humanitarian and faith oriented. We are cosmopolitan and energetic. We have the opportunity to raise a gold standard for the nation. We need to solve some of our problems so that all Dallas citizens have access to education, economic opportunity and a higher quality of life.

LYNN WYATT

The daughter of Bernard Sakowitz and Ann Baum as well as the sister of Robert T. Sakowitz, Lynn Wyatt is a Houston socialite and philanthropist. Her grandfather started the Sakowitz department store chain. Her husband, Oscar Wyatt, is an energy executive. During the oil boom in the 1970s and early 1980s, their home in Houston's River Oaks neighborhood was known as the "Wyatt Hyatt," becoming the preferred Houston residence for Princess Margaret of England, Princess Grace of Monaco, Mick Jagger, Bill Blass, Joan Collins and his Majesty King Hussein and Queen Noor of Jordan.

I have great pride and passion about being a third-generation Texan. Even at the young age of nine at summer camp in Maine, my campmates' eyes grew as large as saucers when they learned I was from Texas. That's when I knew Texas was really special. Houston is an embodiment of the spirit, energy, acceptance and openness that we as a city value. It is truly a unique combination of qualities.

HOUSTON: *River Oaks Country Club*

Culturally we are blessed with world-class art institutions managed by first-class directors, a top medical center known throughout the world, and of course that independent, can-do spirit of Houstonians who refuse to lose. Houston has a flame that just keeps blazing. It's the people of this great city who give me the spark to continue contributing in any way that I can.

Houston is definitely an aspirational city. Greatness aspires greatness. Houstonians have a soaring desire to create anew and still appreciate the past we have been given. I think the arts reflect the soul of a city, and Houston is blessed with a body of excellence in the arts. Houston Grand Opera, Museum of Fine Arts Houston, Houston Ballet, the Menil Collection, the Rothko Chapel are all world-renowned and world-class institutions. Lucky us! The people of Houston offer an openness to new ideas and a great way of life that reflects the energy our city exudes.

I think Houston is a great base. It has stability. It's the energy capital of the world, which brings another complete asset to this city. It has an infusion of entertaining things to do. However, we must look beyond the narrow circle that surrounds us. Even if one lived in Paradise, one must leave it once in a while to be reminded of the good. I've had a lot of fun in Dallas and have great memories of Nancy Harmon's famous parties.

CAROLYN FARB

It's difficult to attend any social event in Houston—and impossible to attend any high-profile event raising money for a good cause—without seeing Carolyn Farb. She set precedents in the art of fundraising for deserving and worthwhile causes in Houston. She received an Honorary Doctorate in Humanities from Northwood University. In addition to her philanthropic work, she is the author of three books, an art collector and a devoted patron of the arts.

I'm a hometown gal and have watched Houston flourish since I was a child growing up in West University. I still love to drive by our family home on Amherst Street to make sure it is still standing.

Houston has become a mega center for oil and gas, energy, medical, health care industries and space. We've gone from our early beginnings as an oil boom town to an international city that the world embraces. When people visit Texas, they are surprised at how sophisticated our city is and all that it has to offer. There is a great quality of life—and a small town charm and warm hospitality that is intoxicating. Houston is the smallest big city which attracts people moving here to take advantage of limitless opportunities.

Houstonians always had a larger than life persona. Being a movie buff, I've never missed an opportunity to watch one of my favorite movies—*Giant*—for the umpteenth time. I remember having fun times in the Olympic-sized swimming pool at the Shamrock Hotel, which was built by the legendary wildcatter Glenn McCarthy. The characters of James Dean as Jett Rink and the Rock Hudson character Bick Benedict, in the novel by Edna Ferber, were one and the same based on the life of Glenn McCarthy.

Houston is constantly evolving and redefining itself. Living here, if you believe in a dream, it can happen. Houston is a city of opportunity for everyone. We enjoy the capacity of hope and believe in the positive energy of fresh starts. If there is a natural disaster in Houston or elsewhere in the country, we are the first to answer the call. In the face of any kind of adversity, Houston is a city that never fails to respond.

Remembering the words of Neil Armstrong, the first man on the moon—"One small step for man; one giant step for mankind." Our rich Texas history is like a magnificent tapestry, and each one of us is part of that ongoing history and future. We benefit from and respect our past.

Houstonians always join together to support a worthy cause. Among many events I have served as chairman. One of the most memorable was in 1983 when Marvin Hamlisch and I raised a million dollars in a single night for The Stehlin Foundation for Cancer Research, which galvanized the community in support of cancer research. That evening Liza Minelli, Ann-Margret, Crystal Gayle, Alan King and Pia Zadora were here and donated their talent. There was magic in the air.

My beloved Houston has provided me the opportunity to take

chances, be innovative, flourish, and to follow my passion of helping others through volunteerism. I believe this is my calling —the great philanthropist Nina Cullinan once told me, I had a special gift to make a difference and impact the lives of others. I'm following her words.

There is no real competition between Houston and Dallas. I cherish my Dallas friends who are changing lives with their charitable and philanthropic organizations. Texas is a great place to live— Dallas retains the charm unique of Texas, but my heart will always be in Houston.

JOAN SCHNITZER-LEVY
Heir to the Weingarten real estate empire in Houston, Joan Schnitzer-Levy knew philanthropy first-hand from an early age. She has worked for many charities over the decades, perhaps most notably the ESCAPE Family Resource Center helping abused children. Since her marriage eighteen years ago, she has divided her time between Houston and Dallas.

My husband is a native Dallasite, and I am a native Houstonian. I've seen much to admire in both cities, though of course I know Houston best. I think the most wonderful thing about Houston is that the people who made money give a big part of it back into the city, whether you look back to Jesse Jones or Gus Wortham or Glenn McCarthy, who built the Shamrock Hotel. There are a lot of rich people in this world, but they don't always give back to make the city better the way Houston always does. People used to think that Houston was all cattle and oil, but we've expanded so much into opera, ballet and museums because the people who had money put it out there. There are always a few people who do this in every city, but here there are many.

In my house growing up, philanthropy was a very big deal. I was lucky I learned. In those days people helped each other and your word was your bond. My father always told me that. You'd borrow $50 million from your bank on a handshake. Of course, those days are long gone. When something was needed, people would call up all their buddies and everybody would pitch in. People who had money would get together, the way they did to build Houston's Medical Center. People have more money now, in terms of zeroes. But they usually do their own thing. It used to be all about getting on the phone. The world is a different world now.

Dallas has done some wonderful things lately. At one time, it was way ahead of Houston in terms of fashion, the arts and things like that, but then we caught up and passed them. Now they've built all these beautiful new buildings and they're catching up with us again. It seems to me that some generations in a city are just more philanthropic than others. Dallas is fortunate to have more people putting money back into the city right now. Take Jerry Jones: He and his wife have done so much for Dallas.

I remember as a little girl asking my father how you know which charity to give to. And he said, "Darlin' there's no such thing as a bad charity. There's just some you like better than others." For me, it's all about children, families and medicine. Every city needs great arts organizations, but I'm always telling people who ask, "These children will never make it to the opera or the ballet if we don't help them now."

JOANNE KING HERRING

Joanne King Herring is a Houston socialite, political activist, businesswoman and former talk show host. In the 1980s she helped convince U.S. Representative Charlie Wilson that Washington should arm and train the resistance fighting against the Soviet Union. This event became the book and finally the movie Charlie Wilson's War, *with Julia Roberts portraying Herring.*

I like to say that Houston is the city of Snap, Crackle and Pop.

Snap: Houston is a city of smart, practical, innovative businesses with opportunities in every sector, no Harvard degree required. Corporations run by men of honor, honesty, faith and family like Jim Hackett and Larry Brookshire. Sustained by good government with freedom from stultifying taxes and regulations and lack of zoning guarded expertly by Mayor Annise Parker.

Crackle: A sparkling restaurant scene, some so avant-garde they are beyond my culinary capability. The others challenge New York and whip the socks off L.A. Wide spectrum of arts from our delicious tunnel at the MFAH and the Rothko chapel to delightful offerings along the bayou and the Art Car Parade. Superlative music: Houston Grand Opera, TUTS, Houston Ballet overseen by Franci Crane and her coterie of caring socialites. Our new bayou park is bigger and better than Central Park—so important to our city and a gift from Nancy and Rich Kinder. According to the *Guinness Book of World Records*, Houston has more trees than any other city. They must be preserved. Every night a grand and glittering fundraiser for great causes, overseen by queen Margaret Williams. Jaguars, Bentleys, Rolls Royces all driven by cute guys and successful women. Fashion fantasia with Tootsies, Bulgari and others providing the flourishes and folderol that has catapulted our glamour queens like Susan Krohn to the pages of international magazines. We are a kaleidoscopic city providing all the color and sparkle of the Land of Oz.

Pop: It all pops when we realize our young still dream of New York City, and we are still not perceived as the cosmopolitan city that we are. In the next years, that will change. Our good economics, if nothing else, will entice the weary world to dance over the rainbow to the pot of gold that is Houston. And where will I be? Up on my cloud with my harp!

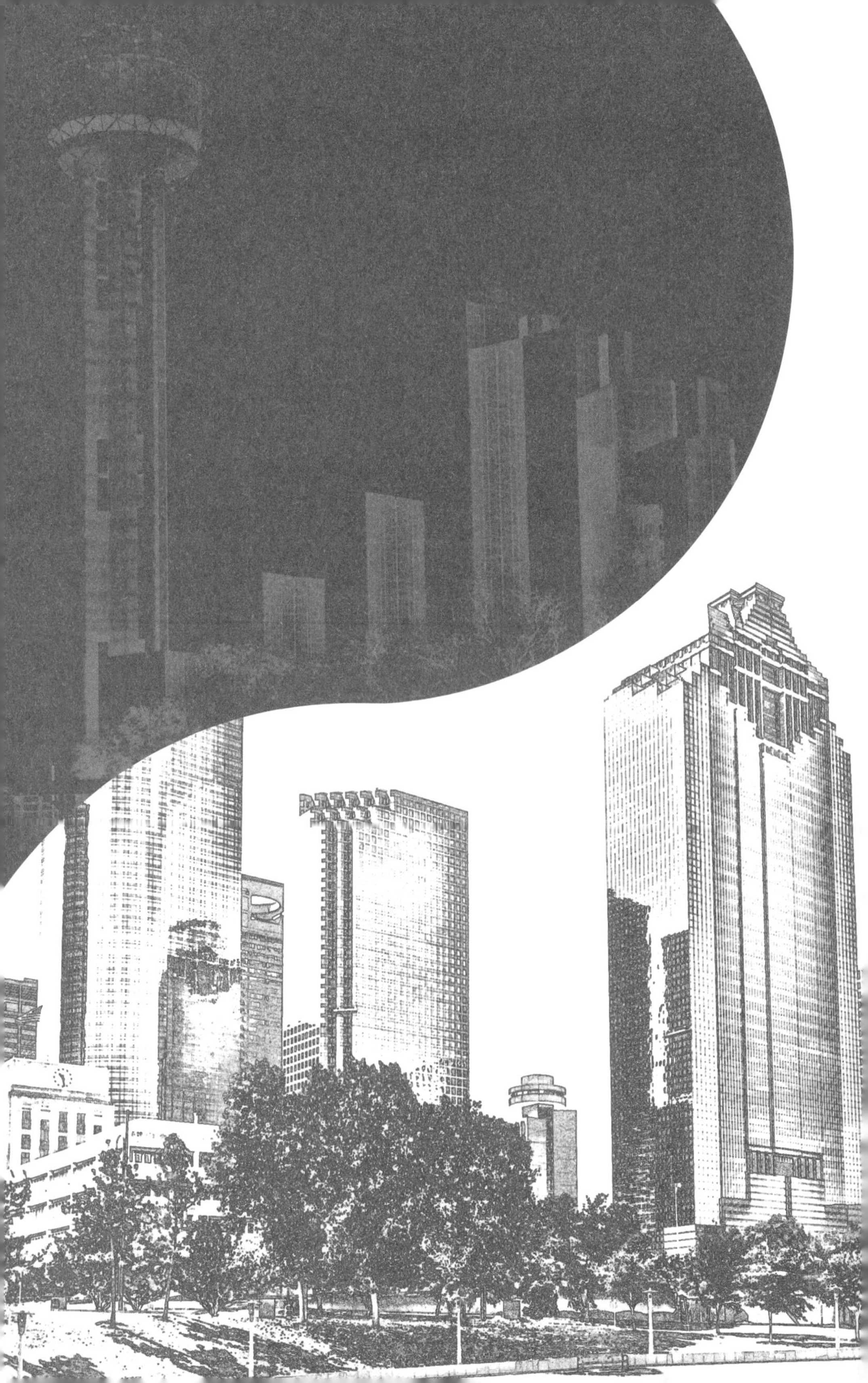

WORSHIP

Most of Texas sits comfortably within what the Deep South likes to call its Bible Belt, meaning it fits culturally as well as theologically. Yet within this broad identity, Dallas and Houston display substantial differences. It seems fair to say that Dallas is more comfortable with its Texas-wide Bible Belt identity than Houston is, primarily because the Gulf Coast city displays a greater diversity of faith traditions—a larger population of immigrants from parts of the world with faiths other than Christianity. In addition, Houstonians are generally *proud* of this fact, since it's a reminder of the study that declared it the "most ethnic" city in America. Both, though, record slightly more declared adherents to some religion than is the national average: 55% in Dallas and 52% in Houston, compared to 50% (or in some studies less) across America.

Dallas and Houston, like the rest of Texas and the rest of the South outside traditionally French-Catholic south Louisiana, are predominantly Protestant, with a population of Southern Baptists, Methodists and evangelicals that's as large as the population of, say, Episcopalians is small. The cities are similar in terms of Catholicism—Houston being home to 14% of the state's Catholics and Dallas to 11%. And, perhaps surprisingly, in terms of Jewish population, Dallas is home to 29% of the Jews living in Texas, and Houston to 28%. Beyond those two, however, things get very different. Houston plays host to 44% of the state's Greek Orthodox population, compared to only 20% for Dallas. Of course, there are several additional Orthodox traditions beyond Greek. A full 41% of the state's Hindus, 40% of the state's Buddhists and 41% of the state's Muslims live in Houston, compared with only 21%, 23% and under 20%, respectively, for those belief systems in Dallas.

DR. ED YOUNG

Dr. H. Edwin Young is the pastor of one of America's largest churches, Second Baptist Church of Houston. During his three decades as pastor, Second has experienced tremendous growth, with a current membership exceeding 65,000. Under his leadership, the church has pioneered the concept of "one church in multiple locations" and currently has six campuses in the greater Houston community. Dr. Young can be seen and heard across North America and throughout the world on Second's broadcast ministry, the Winning Walk. He and his wife, Jo Beth, have three grown sons, all of whom also serve in ministry. Dr. and Mrs. Young have eleven of the world's greatest grandchildren.

Though Houston has grown rapidly into an international city, it still exudes a warm spirit with a receptivity that is uniquely open, evoking an old-town atmosphere. Though we have a diverse and robust economy, our diversity of people is our true wealth. Almost everyone here is from somewhere else. People from all over the world

HOUSTON: *Antioch Missionary Baptist Church Downtown Houston*

have come to Houston, and we have embraced them and made them feel welcome. Instead of an elitist atmosphere that looks inward, Houstonians look outward, offering support and hospitality to newcomers and new ideas.

Exemplifying the forward-thinking spirit for which Houston has become known, the city's founding fathers had the foresight to let us grow geographically without the limitations of zoning laws. People from all over the planet have brought their skills, talents, perspectives and dreams to this vast city that stretches far beyond the banks of the Buffalo Bayou where our founding fathers first landed.

I attended the 150th birthday celebration of Houston and heard a story told by Leon Jaworski that has stuck with me all these years. Apparently, when the Allen Brothers founded Houston they stated, "We want to establish a city 'which has foundations, whose builder and maker is God.'" Mr. Jaworski went on to say the brilliance of the city is that we have stayed close to the foundation laid by the Allen Brothers. We continue to build on that foundation today. It is the same foundation that provides openness to conversations about God and faith. In Houston there is still an openness to the Gospel.

DR. TOM PACE

Thomas J. Pace III is senior pastor of St. Luke's United Methodist Church in Houston. Prior to his appointment to St. Luke's, Tom was the senior pastor of Christ United Methodist Church in Sugar Land, founding pastor at Bay Harbour United Methodist Church on the south shore of Clear Lake, and pastor of Faith United Methodist Church in South Houston.

Because of our entrepreneurial spirit and can-do attitude, Houston has been called the most global city in the United States. Nowhere is that more evident than in the Sharpstown/Gulfton neighborhood surrounding St. Luke's Gethsemane Campus. When St. Luke's United Methodist Church, located in center of Houston, merged with Gethsemane United Methodist Church in 2009, church leaders began asking, "What kind of church will we be? Can we really be the hands and feet of Jesus in this neighborhood? Can we make a positive impact in our city?"

St. Luke's is committed to turning the church inside-out and living out its mission to be "gathered by Jesus to enact faith in love." That is why the church founded Christian Community Service Center in 1978. That organization is now a coalition of 41 churches offering services such as the food pantry that is located on the St. Luke's Gethsemane Campus. Over the past five years, the food pantry has provided food, (including fresh produce from their community garden) to 95,000 hungry Houstonians.

In 2012, Houston: reVision was created through an innovative partnership between St. Luke's United Methodist Church and St. Martin's Episcopal Church. Today reVision is housed at the St. Luke's Gethsemane Campus where church members partner with the Harris County Juvenile Probation Department to provide mentors and positive role models to gang affected youth.

It is through partnerships such as these that St. Luke's continues its tradition of outreach in the city and building the kingdom of God.

RABBI ROY WALTER

Roy A. Walter was born in Memphis but has spent the bulk of his rabbinical career at Congregation Emanu El in Houston, where he has served as assistant and associate rabbi, senior rabbi and now rabbi emeritus. He has participated in many interfaith community initiatives and is also on the faculty of the University of St. Thomas.

One of the things that's important to say is that there is a harmony—not to say we don't have disagreements—but a harmony throughout the Jewish community in Houston, whether Orthodox, Reform or Conservative, that overcomes our differences. I think there's something very Texas about that, in the sense that Texas retains a certain kind of frontier ambiance. On the frontier, sharing with your community is essential to survival, so Texas has this powerful sense of community. One of the things I love about Houston is that we don't care if you're a newcomer or a longtimer. If you want to step up and make the world a better place, we say *come on*. This translates well to the Jewish community, both in terms of our openness to each other and the city's overall openness to us. If you're making a better community, just about nobody here cares about your skin color or your religion.

In Houston as elsewhere, Jews tend to live in Jewish neighborhoods because communities preserve your heritage. But the world we live in now is a lot broader than that. There are, of course, certain issues that Jews and Christians and Muslims disagree on, but the fact is that there are many values that are shared. When you work with people of other faiths to build the community, you demonstrate in real life the theory that by working with you I understand you. We will not allow our differences to prevent us from working together on the values we share. For a synagogue or a church to live its true mission, I believe its work cannot end at the boundaries of its property.

People who receive the food and clothing we donate almost never live in my neighborhood, and they're seldom members of my synagogue. But you serve those people because your religious tradition tells you to feed the hungry, clothe the naked, house the homeless. The fact that they don't live in my neighborhood doesn't mean they're not my neighbor.

There were Jews in Texas from the time of the earliest Spanish land grants. Beth Israel, right here in Houston since in the mid-1800s, is the oldest synagogue in Texas. The first Jews here were Spanish, but the wave of Jewish immigration in the mid-19th century was German and the huge one at the end of that century was Russian and Eastern European. These last, fleeing the pogroms, joined the general flow of immigrants to America, right alongside Italians, Irish, Greeks and just about everybody else. More recently, Houston's Jewish population grew notably at the close of World War II, when veterans came back to live in Texas after serving on military bases here, and again beginning in 1978. Houston was booming then. Jews were among the many who came here for economic reasons.

In Houston, as in many large American cities, it's often noted that Jews do more in terms of philanthropy than our numbers would suggest—funding hospitals, schools, libraries and other things that contribute to the public good. Really, it all comes down to a very basic question: Who are Jews and what do we believe on the everyday level? Our tradition teaches us that whatever salvation is, it is earned by deeds. Judaism is very interested in behavior. Rabbis talk a lot more about doing the right thing—doing what God expects of you—than about believing the right thing. The last line of our prayer for Yom Kippur calls for penance, prayer and charity. That's how you get inscribed in the Book of Life. And it doesn't mean just giving money or goods. It means giving of yourself.

DALLAS: *Cathedral Santuario de Guadalupe*

ROBERT JEFFRESS

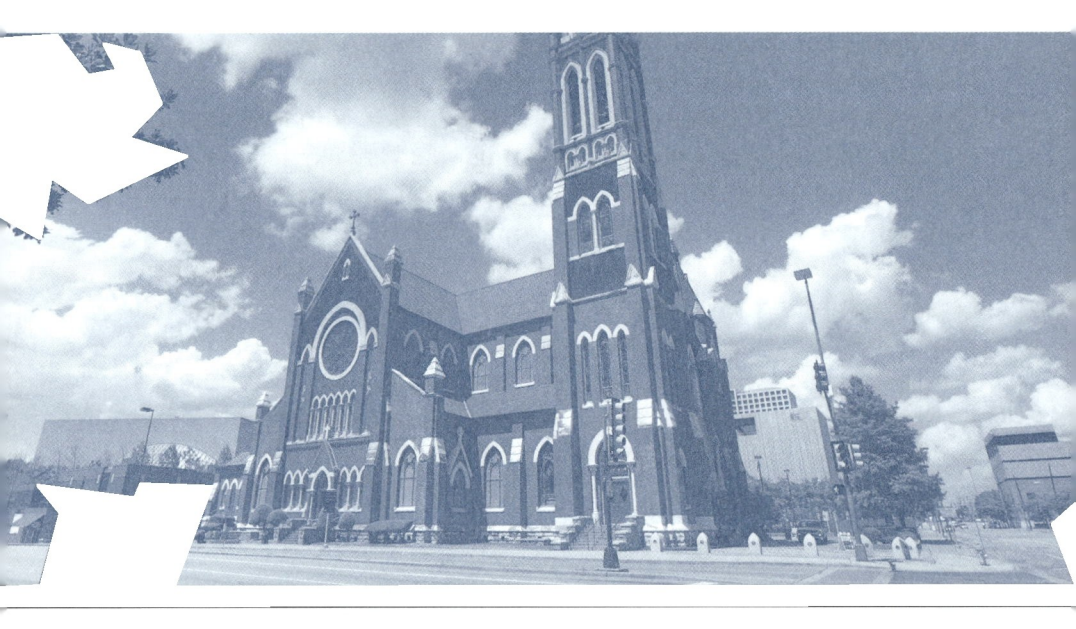

Dr. Robert Jeffress is the senior pastor of the 11,000-member First Baptist Church of Dallas, which he has served on his hometown since August 2007. He graduated from Southwestern Theological Seminary with a D.Min., after earning a Th.M. from Dallas Theological Seminary and a B.S. degree from Baylor University. In May 2010, he was awarded a Doctor of Divinity degree from Dallas Baptist University.

It's often said that the Southwest is the Bible Belt. If that is true, Dallas is the buckle of the Bible Belt. For most of the past century, Dallas has been a center of evangelical faith. And Dallas remains friendly to any Christian, despite recent increases in the diversity of faiths we have in this city. As a result, Dallas has become home to some major Christian organizations and some premier Christian churches. Beyond what we do at First Baptist, there's Tony Evans at Oak Cliff, Chuck Swindoll north of Dallas (in Frisco), and Ed Young Jr. of Fellowship Church in Grapevine. I don't know of any other city in America that has so many prominent Christian organizations and churches. Historically, there's a certain conservative tone to Dallas that makes it fertile ground for evangelical Christianity. It's a place that attracts Christian entities, if you will.

I grew up in Dallas. In fact, I grew up at First Baptist Church. I went away for 22 years of pastoral duties, first in Eastland and then at a large church in Wichita Falls, and then I came home, which means I can see all the changes. In general, we live in a much more secular society now. When I was growing up, going to church was the socially expected thing to do. It's become much more socially acceptable to not go to church on Sundays and to not express yourself using a Christian vocabulary. I personally think that's a good thing. I think there ought to be a character distinction between those who are followers of Christ and those who aren't. Here in Dallas, I believe faith really does impact how people conduct their business and personal lives. There are Bible studies held regularly. For people of faith, Christianity extends far beyond what happens in church on Sunday.

I think people love what's still considered the hospitable and friendly atmosphere of our city. People who visit or move here are always struck by the hospitality. A lot of people also appreciate the independent streak we have here in Dallas—the way we are not always politically correct in every situation. That's part of our Texas brand as well. People at First Baptist appreciate being in a church in which people really care for each other. We have a lot more diversity now, though, than we had when I was growing up—socially, ethnically. We had a dinner last night for several hundred prospects, and I'd say half of them were Hispanic. And we've started offering Spanish translations of our services.

I think Dallas is on a good path. Our former mayor is a member of our church, and he did a lot of good things while he was in office. Probably our weakest link is the Dallas Independent School District. Our church has a private school, but there are many, many residents who can't afford a private school. My mom taught in Dallas for thirty years, and I don't believe any city is going to reach its full potential without a world-class public school system.

RECTOR ROBERT DANNALS

After growing up where Florida meets Georgia along the coast and gaining pastoral experience in the Carolinas, Bob Dannals has been rector of St. Michael and All Angels Episcopal Church in the Park Cities area of Dallas since 2007. He is a Graduate Theological, and a graduate of Florida State University, Virginia Theological Seminary and Drew University.

Dallas is pretty intense. People say it's kind of hardwired and very energetic. When they know the places I've been in my life, they always ask me what Dallas is like, and I say it's kind of a cross between Atlanta and Charlotte and Beverly Hills. There's a part of Dallas that's definitely larger than life. It's a can-do city with a can-do spirit, and it's a lot more international than most people realize. One of the largest Ethiopian communities in America is right here in Dallas. Who would have thought that Dallas would be so attractive to Ethiopians? There's a large Asian population, and of course a huge Hispanic population like everywhere in Texas. And there's a large and active African-American community, just like there is in Houston.

Since I grew up in the Deep South, I see Texas as part of the Deep South, too. I know, if you ask a Texan if this is the South, they say *no, it's Texas.* There's a feeling that this is a region unto itself, and if you've ever driven from Dallas down to the Rio Grande Valley or maybe Dallas to El Paso, you know that the place is big enough to be a region unto itself. But still, there are things about Texas—wide-open country and friendly people—that I see as Southern. If you are conscientious and have a giving spirit, Dallas is ready for you to get involved.

Our congregation is mostly white, partly because of where we're located in the Park Cities and partly because Episcopalians have traditionally been mostly white. But we are becoming more diverse all the time. And we are involved in a lot of places in Dallas. Our core values come from the Gospel. Christians are usually driven by the teachings of Jesus and our traditions, whether we're Episcopalians or Methodists or Baptists or Catholics. If we are attentive to our faith, we'll be involved with people who are not like us, people who are poor, people who are left out. We are supposed to go and do as Jesus did. And there are a lot of faith communities doing just the same as we are. Dallas is a very generous and sharing community, whether we are Christians or Jews or Muslims. We are not interested in this because of some liberal consciousness or to put another notch in our own belt. We're interested because of concern for people who have somehow been left out.

For all of our challenges in this city, from unemployment to hunger to homelessness, we have a robust business community, and we need to continue to have that. We still have areas of racism that need our attention, and gender conflict. We want to continue to advance in the areas of inclusion, whether that means people of color, men and women, straight and gay, or diversity of income. Especially for the faith community, these differences all add up to a challenge that can become an opportunity.

MARK YARBROUGH

Dr. Mark Yarbrough serves as vice-president for academic affairs, academic dean and assistant professor of Bible exposition at Dallas Theological Seminary. His undergraduate degree is from Dallas Christian College, where he was named valedictorian.

In the early 1920s, when our founder was looking at starting a seminary, he looked first at educational institutions that had all been founded on training individuals for the ministry—places like Harvard, Yale and Princeton. But he could see, even back then, that those institutions in the Northeast were moving away from their own heritage founded on the word of God, the Bible. There were, on the other hand, some strong connections to some good churches in the Dallas area, and that led to formation of a board and then opening of Dallas Theological Seminary in 1924. So there was a need in the Dallas area, one that was addressed in association with others who identified that need.

Dallas is still part of the Bible Belt, still a conservative place for families and for social activities, and you can still get a sense of its early days as part of the South. We have lots of prospective students who are moving here from all over the country, and I tell them they'll see things here on the streets of Dallas—hospitality, friendly smiles, howdies from people—that they may not see in the cities and towns they're coming here from. These things were once common in this country, but they've been lost in many cities.

There is no doubt that here in Dallas the aspect of worship is very, very important. There are many excellent churches, many of them pastored by our graduates, and attendance is more than a perfunctory hour on Sunday morning. It filters down into how we do business, into a genuine concern for how we treat other people, whether they're customers or employees. One of the claims of Christianity is that it's not just what you say you believe but how you live. It's one of the heartbeats of our faith. You are supposed to see the impact of the church in culture. It's supposed to matter if a business owner is a man or woman of faith.

Since I'm a third-generation Dallasite, I've seen a lot of changes. I grew up in a small community closer to Fort Worth, where you could go dove hunting in your backyard. That certainly isn't the case anymore. The city has become a major transportation hub. It has evolved in association with our major sporting events. It has become a place for conventions, especially in the winter when travel to the Northeast is often a problem. We have reliable weather here in the winter in general. No one wants to be here in July, when we burn to a crisp.

The seminary's expansion to Houston in 1990 came about in connection with some of graduates working there, whether in ministry or in the business community. We saw an opportunity there, a need, and DTS-Houston is now the largest seminary program in Houston. We see some interesting things, including the number of students from Hispanic, Asian or other ethnic backgrounds. Churches in Houston are dealing in a very good way with multi-cultural congregations. And what we see in Houston now is what we expect to see in Dallas with the 2020 census. We are thrilled, and we are happy to learn.

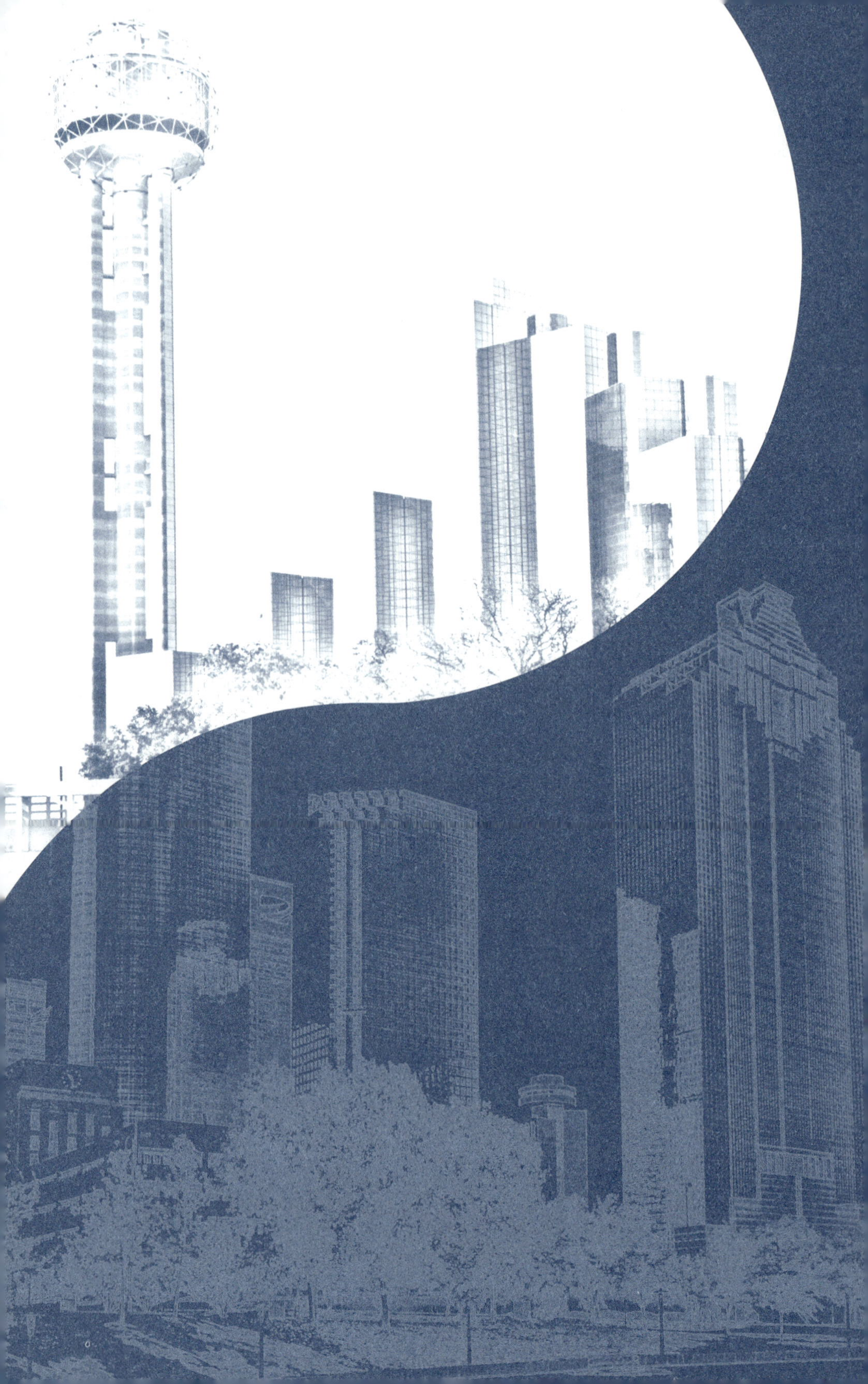

04

ARTS & CULTURE

From the early years of the 20th century, as Houston and Dallas emerged from the stark, deprivational frontier lifestyles with which they were formed, there was general agreement among the cities' leaders that arts and culture were what made a city great. At the start, there was no organized body of researching pointing to the weight given by corporations to opera or symphony or museums when seeking to relocate—only the awareness that the cities that had to be beaten had such things. East Coast culture capitals like New York and Boston had histories longer than Texas could match, so Houston and Dallas began applying the one philosophy, the one methodology that has always served Texas well: Bigger is better.

Throughout the latter years of the 20th century, the two cities aspired to measure arts and culture with numbers, creating larger arts museums with more blockbuster exhibits, larger opera houses and symphony halls hosting more high-profile, big-name, big-bucks performances and larger numbers of seats gathered into some sort of Theater District. Houston in particular came to shine in this department, boasting of the most theater seats in one district outside of New York. By the time the early 21st century rolled around, Dallas was more than ready to steal some ink, building and promoting what may be the most beautiful and largest Arts District in America.

In the grand scheme of things, however, arts and culture need to be about more than buildings, which of course are all about money—something the two largest cities in Texas have managed to hold onto better than most cities in the United States through some very austere times. Both cities have maintained and even expanded their marquee cultural treasures while also encouraging smaller arts organizations devoted to very new dance, very old music and some theater that might make a lot of people mad. Such is the nature of arts and culture: there has to be something for everybody.

GARY TINTEROW

A native Houstonian, Gary Tinterow spent 40 years on the East Coast in college, graduate school and some very prominent museums before the call came to come home. He served as a high-profile curator at New York's Metropolitan Museum of Art until accepting the top job at the Museum of Fine Arts Houston in 2011.

I grew up in Braeswood, a child of two native Texans. My father was BOI in Galveston and my mother, Ann Richards' first cousin, came from Hico, Texas. Throughout my childhood, I commuted between those very different worlds of a declining, slightly tawdry Galveston; dusty, dry (no alcohol) West Texas; and booming, gleaming Houston. When I left Houston in 1972 for college in Boston, I had no reason to think I would ever return: I wanted to live in the East. But when the opportunity arose to work at the MFAH, I was thrilled and never hesitated for a second. I had come to realize that my career and destiny were formed in Houston, that I was a product of this environment, and I was finally ready to return. Ours is a great

HOUSTON: *Museum of Fine Arts*

museum with marvelous trustees, tremendously talented staff, and an informed and committed audience. There's a great deal of untapped potential here in Houston, with an impressive and growing presence in the cultural sphere.

As a child, when I started to notice such things, I was struck by how international a community Houston was. Because of the oil and gas industry and the medical center, we attract people from Norway to Nigeria, from India to Indonesia. We are a port city and we have always been open to outsiders. Other than the oil crisis in the early 1980s, it seemed that the city was on a 45-degree ascent of affluence and ambition. Houstonians, from Jesse Jones and Ima Hogg, Oveta Culp Hobby and Roy Cullen, to Dominique and John de Menil and Audrey Jones Beck, always wanted the best, to do things in the best possible way. Perhaps a dozen families were constantly investing to ensure that we had magnificent cultural offerings. It is marvelous that those founding families are still here in force, and that their children and grandchildren are still leaders in the arts and philanthropy. Whether it's a cultural or civic building, or a medical facility, there are five or six foundations whose names still grace the top of every donor list. With their help, our arts institutions are mature, secure and operating at the very highest level of quality.

I want Houston to continue along this path, and so I hope to promote a greater awareness of our cultural amenities. We have a cultural infrastructure here that rivals Boston, Chicago, San Francisco and Los Angeles, but we are not yet a tourist destination. We are thought of as a business town, a corporate headquarters, which of course we are, just shy of New York in the number of Fortune 500 corporations based here. But I don't think it's widely understood what Houston offers in terms of cultural amenities and overall quality of life. That's going to be key in the years ahead, whether we are talking about bicycle trails, public art, theaters, museums, hospitals or sports arenas. The people we most want to attract to Houston can choose to live anywhere. For us to remain competitive with other cities, we have to make sure our quality of life is up to snuff. And happily, change is visible everywhere. More and more, our light rail is connecting places so visitors can get safely and conveniently to all the major hubs—NRG Stadium, the Medical Center, the Museum District, downtown.

More and more, people are voting with their feet, living close to work, walking and biking rather than driving.

I used to visit Dallas a great deal, and it always seemed to me very different from Houston. It felt like it was on the verge of the Great Plains, in the center of the country, in contrast to Houston, which seemed poised on the edge of the world. My friends in Dallas were decidedly American in their outlook, looking inward for the culture. Here in Houston, we were always very conscious that there is a larger, quite varied world out there to discover. But it must be said that both cities have changed enormously over the last half-century, very much for the better. Urbanistically, culturally, economically, Houston and Dallas are both on a roll.

MARK HANSON

A Boston native, Mark C. Hanson is executive director/CEO of the Houston Symphony. While a participant in the League of American Orchestras' orchestra management fellowship program, Hanson trained at the Houston Symphony, as well as at the New York Philharmonic and the Syracuse Symphony. He began his undergraduate studies as a cellist at the Eastman School of Music, transferring to Harvard to earn a bachelor's in social studies.

Growing up in Boston, I had always heard that Houstonians were very friendly, social, forward-thinking and ambitious. Both my wife Christina's experiences as a student at Rice University's Shepherd School of Music and my own experiences as a management fellow with the Houston Symphony in the late 1990s confirmed this reputation. Since Day One of my second association with the Houston Symphony, we have found our interactions with the people of Houston to be most enjoyable.

As the Houston Symphony begins its second century, we continue to depend upon and benefit from the engagement of and the generosity of thousands and thousands of culturally-aware Houstonians. Because of this, Houston has all of the attributes needed to support a world-class symphony orchestra as well as a growing citywide arts scene. I haven't met a single person in Houston who doesn't expect that tomorrow will be a better day than yesterday. It's simply how people are wired in this great city. As artists, our musicians have been guided by this same philosophy from the moment they dedicated their lives to mastering their own musical instruments and to perfecting their performance as an ensemble. I have never before experienced so much quality built over so many decades, mixed with so much ambition for a brighter future.

During our multi-faceted centennial season, the Houston Symphony looked back and looked forward while celebrating its past and launching its future. We wanted to celebrate one hundred years of great performances and the talented music directors, musicians, staff and board members who have made our first century possible. But we also sought to use the centennial season as our launching pad for what we know will be an even more remarkable second century! What has helped the Houston Symphony get here is a deeply ingrained desire to be the best, internationally renowned symphony orchestra for Houston as possible. You might not expect to find a symphony of this quality in a city that's still quite young, especially by the standards of East Coast or European music capitals, where orchestras go back a couple of centuries.

We are also re-examining how this institution relates to our city as a whole. We want to become culturally indispensable to as many people as possible throughout this growing, diverse community. We want to gain as many new fans of symphonic music as possible, whether they come for our concerts in Jones Hall or our concerts throughout the community. We want to reach people who haven't had the opportunity or the desire up to this point in their lives to hear orchestral music performed by 87 talented and dedicated musicians.

We are an incredibly flexible symphony orchestra. We can provide performances—especially through our pops, family and neighborhood concerts—that appeal to all of Houston's diverse citizenry, without compromising our core classical concerts or alienating our core classical audiences who have sustained us for so long. We remain deeply committed to the trans-formative power of these timeless classical masterworks. Yet, there's really nothing out there in the musical universe that we can't perform, from jazz to big band to rock to mariachi to contemporary pop. Our competitive advantage as a cultural service provider, as an entertainment form and as an educational institution is that we can perform concerts that connect us with so many different people and cultures. We have a huge opportunity to spread this message out to everybody in Houston and to contribute to Houston's ongoing growth as an international and inter-connected city.

PATRICK SUMMERS

Patrick Summers is artistic and music director of Houston Grand Opera (HGO), having served as music director since 1998, and principal guest conductor of the San Francisco Opera (SFO). Over the past decade, Mr. Summers has led many of HGO's artistic and strategic initiatives, including initiating its own orchestra and founding HGOco, the company's groundbreaking educational/outreach program to the Houston community.

I love both Houston and Dallas, though Houston does, in my view, feel more international and diverse, two qualities that I love. Dallas feels very Texan, which I love; Houston feels like a world city. Houston is a place where great ideas get done, and the great idea is taken and evaluated for its own sake, not based on schooling, family or wealth. There is plenty of conspicuous consumption in both Houston and Dallas, but Houston feels more like a "can-do" place, whereas Dallas feels more judgmental based on surface factors. I have no scientific basis for this; it's just a feeling.

I'm simply trying to give Houston the arts company it says it wants, which is a multifarious place dedicated not only to great opera, but to connecting with our community at deep levels and telling their stories through music, which is what opera is. Though I work around the world, Houston has been the heart of my artistic life for the past decade or more, and I've loved it.

Oil has always defined the booms and busts of Houston, and it continues to do so. The fortunes of the arts companies in the city have always followed that. On most days, Houston is a city where your great idea can find traction. Just be clear, open, and leave your haughtiness at the door, please. We are much more open and progressive than one might think, given the cultural clichés about Texas. Vibrant. Bold. Fun. Interesting. Unexpected. And growing.

We have the worst drivers on earth and the summer weather is horrible. The winter weather is gorgeous, though, but I wish that helped the driving; it doesn't. Dallas is geographically more interesting and attractive than Houston. But they have the same aggressive and terrifying drivers we do!

NANCY WOZNY
Nancy Wozny is editor of Arts + Culture Texas *magazine. An upstate New York native who adopted Texas (and vice versa) years ago, Nancy loves all the arts but has a special affection for classical ballet, modern dance and many things in between.*

The sheer amount of artistic activity going on in Houston across all the art forms is amazing. There are so many choices at so many levels. I love the way Houston artists think big. Who would have thought that a small dance organization would build a state-of-the-art studio? Who would have thought that small troupes would get national attention?

I have probably written more about Houston arts organizations and artists than any other person—most of them good. I wrote of numerous artists in national publications, including Houston Ballet principal Karina Gonzalez's cover story in *Dance* magazine and Melissa Hough's cover story in *Pointe*. I selected Joseph Walsh as one to watch when he was a student, and now he is a principal dancer with Houston Ballet. I have a good eye for talent and have gotten several artists national exposure. As writers, we want to follow artists who are doing important work. I have been lucky to be able to chronicle many artists who are doing work that matters.

In Houston, I loved when Annise Parker proclaimed dance as her favorite art form at a panel of mayoral candidates. She got my vote. As for Dallas seen from Houston, it's a long drive but there is a tremendous amount of arts there, too.

CATHERINE CUELLAR

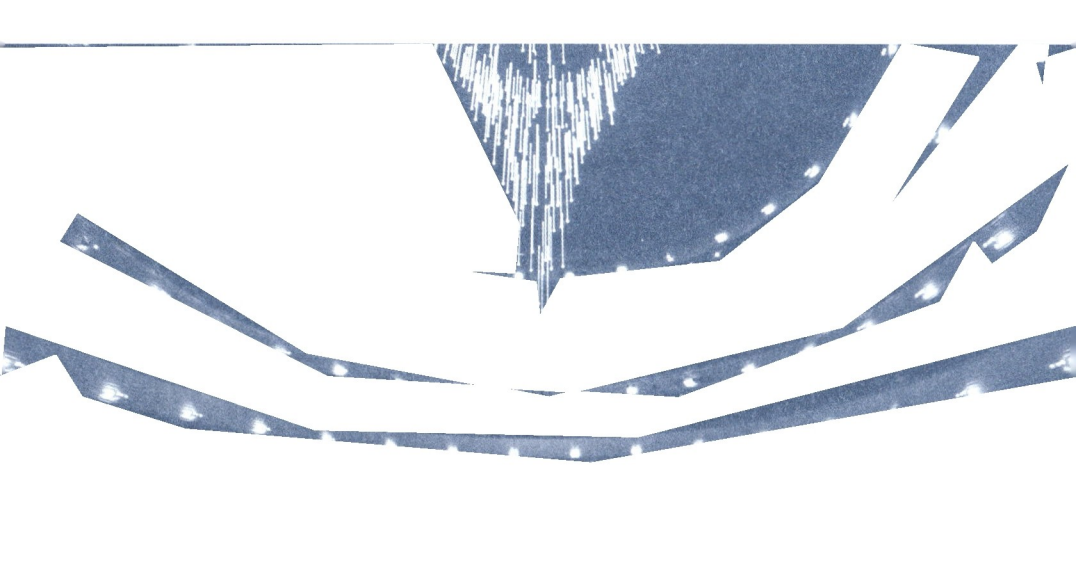

Catherine Cuellar is executive director of the Dallas Arts District. Her grandfather and his brothers started El Chico, which grew to be the largest Latino franchiser in the U.S. With a sixth grade education, her grandfather Frank X. Cuellar was the first Latino to serve on the Dallas Citizens Council. Her cousin Mariano Martinez invented the frozen margarita in Dallas.

The Dallas Arts District has flipped a giant switch on urban revitalization, attracting millions of new visitors to downtown. The Dallas Museum of Art is the first museum of scale in the U.S. to offer free membership and free admission. We boast more buildings by Pritzker Prize-winning architects than any neighborhood. Norman Foster's Winspear Opera House has been named the best in America by *Opera* magazine, and the Dallas Opera's schedule allows fans to enjoy back-to-back weekend performances featuring Grammy-winning cast members.

DALLAS: *Winspear Opera House*

The Crow Collection of Asian Art celebrated its fifteenth anniversary in 2013 with the grand reopening of its sculpture garden. The new Dallas City Performance Hall has featured concerts by UNT's Grammy-nominated One O'Clock Lab Band and one of the nation's premiere gay men's choruses, the Turtle Creek Chorale, as well as world premieres by Undermain Theatre (Obie Award-winning Len Jenkin's *Abraham Zobell's Home Movie: Final Reel*) and late Dallas choreographer Bruce Wood (*RED+2* and *TOUCH*). Dallas Independent School District's Booker T. Washington High School for the Performing and Visual Arts has been named among the top public schools in the nation and had five of its 2014 graduates accepted to The Juilliard School.

The Dallas Theater Center earned recognition from First Lady Michele Obama for Project Discovery, the best after-school program in the nation, and opened two world-premiere musicals that continued to New York in 2014: *Fly by Night* and *Fortress of Solitude*. Our new Klyde Warren Park also connects the new Perot Museum of Nature and Science, which sold more than a million tickets in its first year.

In traveling on five continents, I've never experienced such a grand and humbling combination of talent, goodwill and generosity. The first phase of the Arts District resulting from decades of vision and planning is now complete, and I am honored to serve its leaders and visitors. Of a half-dozen new construction projects now in-flight or soon to break ground, I'm most excited by La Reunion TX's Flora Lofts, which will create affordable housing for working artists and their families in the Arts District, scheduled to open in 2015.

With the 2012 opening of the Dallas City Performance Hall, Klyde Warren Park, and the Perot Museum of Nature and Science exceeding expectations, coupled with the Dallas Museum of Art's return to free admission and launch of free membership in 2013, millions are visiting downtown and creating wonderful memories. In June 2014, the Dallas Arts District hosted the North American debut of the New Cities Summit, welcoming 800 entrepreneurs, scholars and government leaders from more than 50 countries, and we now serve as world headquarters of the Global Cultural Districts Network. Another defining moment was in 2006, when half a million people peacefully marched from Catedral Santuario de Guadalupe through downtown to City Hall on Palm Sunday urging comprehensive immigration reform.

Dallas' history is amazing; we don't just have artifacts in museums. We have living history. In 2015, the Dallas Symphony Orchestra will celebrate the first annual *Soluna* festival, *Destination America,* featuring indoor and outdoor exhibits and performances throughout the Dallas Arts District during the month of May. Fair Park comprises the largest collection of intact Art Deco architecture in the U.S. The Dallas Black Dance Theatre building was a YMCA where Muhammad Ali, Thurgood Marshall, Dr. Martin Luther King, Jr. and Ella Fitzgerald stayed before integration of Dallas' hotels. St. Paul United Methodist Church was built in 1873 by freed slaves for whom it was illegal to read and write, but their hand-carved wooden support beams and hand-laid bricks stand to this day, and they have hosted a free concert series, *Tuesday Nite Jazz,* for 17 years. With the addition of non-stop flights to Hong Kong and Shanghai, China, and Doha, Qatar, and the opening of a new DART light rail station at DFW airport in 2014, we can only imagine what the future holds, but know our Arts District will help Dallasites to creatively embrace it.

BEN STEVENSON

Born in 1936, Ben Stevenson, OBE, is a former ballet dancer with Britain's Royal Ballet and English National Ballet, co-director of National Ballet of Washington from 1971 to 1974, artistic director of Chicago Ballet from 1974 to 1975, artistic director of Houston Ballet from 1976 to 2003 and current artistic director of Texas Ballet Theater based in Fort Worth.

There are so many things that have been achieved to make Dallas one of America's most outstanding cities. Many of these occurred before my time here, but the growth in the performing arts has been particularly exciting to me personally. Something new seems to be happening all the time—not only in dance but also with Dallas' amazing opera, symphony, theater groups and museums. Of course the city's love of sports makes for an interesting mix, and we'd better not forget the extraordinary Texas hospitality.

I feel a great amount of excitement and anticipation about the new AT&T Performing Arts Center. The Winspear Opera House (the crown jewel), accompanied by the Wyly Theater, City Performing Hal and the Skokos outdoor stage in the Annette Straus performing space and the Klyde Warren Park performing space give the city five new performance spaces, a great gift for all the performing arts.

I do think that the city is aspirational in the way that its people have a love for its development with a keen eye on the future. It has a very special go-ahead feel with its restaurants, arts, sports, museums, businesses and sense of community. Dallas is very eclectic and is able to interest so many people, making it an extremely desirable place to live. People come from all over to live in this vibrant city and contribute to its uniqueness. Texas is full of exciting cities, with Houston, Austin, Fort Worth and Dallas all being heavyweights in the performing arts.

KEVIN MORIARTY

In September 2007, Kevin Moriarty became Dallas Theater Center's sixth artistic director, leading the company into the Rem Koolhaus-designed Dee and Charles Wyly Theatre in the new Dallas Center for the Performing Art. From 1959 to 2009, the theater was based in the Kalita Humphreys Theater designed by Frank Lloyd Wright.

Dallas is very supportive of new work. Several of our biggest hits and most beloved works have been new works, including *Fly by Night* and *Fly*. I think Dallas audiences love seeing work at Dallas Theater Center that starts here and then later ends up on Broadway or at theaters across the country. Instead of just receiving tours of the best work from New York, Dallas can now serve as a home for the creation of new work and contribute to the national dialogue.

As an art form, the theater requires great writers to continue to create new work that speaks directly to a contemporary audience. If this stops, and all we're left with is the great classics from the past, then theater as an art form will calcify and slowly die as it becomes disconnected from the times and places in which we live. Luckily, we are currently in an age when we are surrounded by great living playwrights writing important new plays. Whether it's bold dramas or popular new musicals, there is a lot of great new writing happening all over the country, and audiences are flocking to it.

Great playwrights respond to the world around them with honesty and a deeply personal connection. I've found that the more specific and personal a writer is about her own life and the times in which she lives, the more universal and lasting the play turns out to be. For instance, Shakespeare wrote very specifically for his Elizabethan audience and was deeply influenced by the world around him, but his plays have lived on for hundreds of years because he touched on universal truths about what it is to be human.

At Dallas Theater Center we're committed to producing new plays and musicals every year. We spend lots of time throughout the year traveling across the country to meet with writers and see productions of their work, and we read hundreds of new plays every year. We commission new plays from the writers who seem most exciting to us. For instance, Kim Rosenstock wrote a play called *Tigers Be Still*, which I saw in New York a few years ago. I thought her voice was fresh and engaging, so we produced a production of *Tigers* at DTC, and then, this year, we produced a new musical she wrote, *Fly by Night*. Now we've commissioned her to write a new play for us in the coming years.

At DTC, we believe that our primary aim in producing plays is to inspire a dialogue with our community about the lives we live—our joys, concerns, and issues that matter to us. Though many classic plays are deeply relevant today, we think it's important that we include new plays in our season because they're most likely to speak directly to our time and place. Also, it's a great joy to have the writers in residence in Dallas for more than a month during the rehearsal process, doing rewrites, providing insights for the actors and directors and engaging with our staff, board and the community at large. We can't do that with a dead writer like Shakespeare!

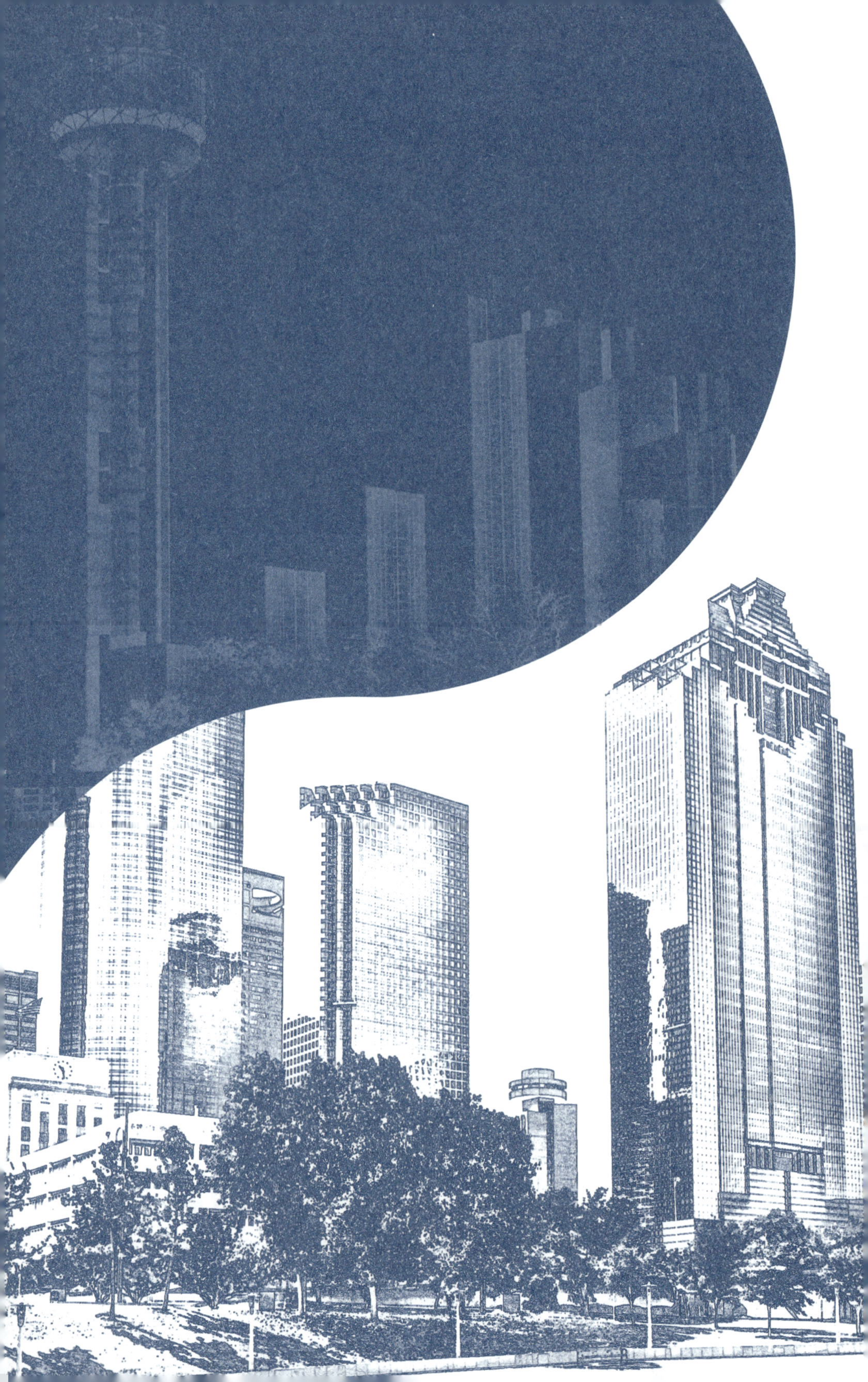

MEDICINE

In the immediate aftermath of World War II, a movement was launched—part science, part fund-raising and part boosterism—that would give Houston the largest medical center not only in Texas or in the country but also in the world. By the start of the 21st century, Houston could report that its Texas Medical Center was a virtual city within a city housing no fewer than fifty medical and medical-related institutions, including fifteen hospitals, two medical schools and four nursing schools. Today, the Medical Center receives upwards of 160,000 visitors each day, with the 18,000 patients from other countries contributing to Houston's reputation as an international city. What's more, the Medical Center employs more than 106,000 people, contributing to the city's vast and vibrant economy.

One of the more interesting sagas within the center's history concerns today's Baylor College of Medicine, which spans 113 years and our two great cities. BCM first started teaching future doctors in Dallas in 1900 and affiliated with Baylor University in Waco three years later. In 1943 it was invited to join the Texas Medical Center in Houston and began its rise to international prominence with the arrival of Dr. Michael DeBakey in 1948. The college separated from Baylor University by mutual agreement in 1969 to become an independent institution. Today Baylor is a health science university with a medical school nationally ranked as one of the top 20 for research by *U.S. News & World Report;* The School for Allied Health Sciences is among the best 10 in the nation; and the Graduate School of Biomedical Sciences is rated in the top 10%. Most recently, in 2014 Baylor St. Luke's Medical Center was announced as a joint venture of Baylor College of Medicine and Catholic Health Initiatives St. Luke's Health.

No one who lives in and/or loves Dallas is inclined to take all these Houston superlatives lying down. Though the numbers from down south are impressive, Dallas and its neighbors in Fort Worth can boast of many terrific medical facilities and more than a few special claims to fame. Parkland Memorial, the city's public hospital, renown for the tens of thousands of patients who owe their lives to its expertise, is also remembered for a historic trio brought there beyond saving. President John F. Kennedy was pronounced dead at Parkland that tragic November 22, 1963, followed by his assassin Lee Harvey Oswald two days later, and followed by Oswald's convicted killer Jack Ruby four years after that.

Today the Dallas-Fort Worth Metroplex is home to 134 hospitals, the most highly regarded being Baylor University Medical Center and UT Southwestern Medical Center in Dallas, along with the Texas Health Harris Methodist Hospital in Fort Worth. In addition to these major and multi-faceted facilities, Dallas is home to at least two specialties that reflect its unique personality. This city of numerous professional sports teams and a notable interest in wellness and fitness is one of the birthplaces of what came to be known as "sports medicine" as well as the birthplace of "aerobics."

DENTON COOLEY, M.D.

Born in 1920, Denton Cooley is an American heart surgeon most famous for performing the first implantation of a completely artificial heart. Cooley is also founder and surgeon-in-chief of the Texas Heart Institute, chief of cardiovascular surgery at St. Luke's Episcopal Hospital, consultant in cardiovascular surgery at Texas Children's Hospital and a clinical professor of surgery at the University of Texas Medical School in Houston. He was awarded the Presidential Medal of Freedom, the nation's highest civilian award, by President Reagan in 1984, and the National Medal of Technology by President Clinton in 1998.

As a native Houstonian, I take special pride in the development of our city. Shortly after the Battle of San Jacinto, the Allen Brothers, who were promoters from New York, laid out the plan for the city using geometric blocks for the downtown area. Houston has enjoyed the original plans, which make the downtown area more orderly than other cities in Texas. Most citizens find personal pride in this

HOUSTON: *Texas Medical Center*

community, have a reputation for philanthropy and hold ambitious visions for the future.

In am fortunate to have participated in the development of the Texas Medical Center as a promoter of the study and treatment of diseases of the heart and blood vessels. The leadership was stimulated by the development of the Texas Heart Institute, where many innovations were introduced, including the first successful transplant of the heart in the United States and the first replacement of the heart with a mechanical device. By establishing the Texas Medical Center, a platform was created for many new procedures in cardiovascular surgery. Today it has become the largest medical center in the world.

One of the most important events in Houston's history occurred nearby in Beaumont with the discovery of oil at Spindletop. The city has become a center for petroleum and chemical plants. The creation of the Space Center in Houston developed a commanding position for future achievement, notably the first lunar landing in 1969. The first word spoken from the moon was "Houston." The city enjoys a favorable geographic location to Latin American countries and we enjoy being an inland seaport. Downtown Dallas was not planned and was defined by early migrants or movement of cattle and wildlife. Dallas has some of the advantages of Atlanta for air travel, but it remains landlocked.

ROBERT C. ROBBINS, M.D.

Internationally recognized cardiac surgeon Robert C. Robbins became president and CEO of the Texas Medical Center in 2012. Prior to that, he was professor and chairman of the Department of Cardiothoracic Surgery at Stanford University School of Medicine, where he served as a member of the faculty since 1993. He served as director of the Stanford Cardiovascular Institute, of the Heart-Lung and Lung Transplantation Programs and of the Cardiothoracic Transplantation Laboratory.

In 1944, the M.D. Anderson Foundation paid about $415,000 to the city of Houston for 134 acres of undeveloped land on the south side of Hermann Park. That is about $3,100 per acre. This land became home to the Texas Medical Center. The Medical Center is now the 8th largest business district in the United States, right after Philadelphia and Seattle. It's home to the largest concentration of medical professionals and experts in the world. Collectively, it's the largest employer in Houston.

Houston Methodist Hospital is the official health care provider for the Houston Texans, the Houston Dynamo, the Houston Astros, the Houston Symphony, the Houston Ballet and Houston Grand Opera. More than 68 babies are born every day in the Texas Medical Center. In the Center, there are more than two hundred separate international collaboration initiatives involving more than five thousand international students, plus 4,000 international workers and visiting scholars. Clinical research in the Texas Medical Center generates an average of 15 new start-up businesses a year and averages a new discover every other day. More heart surgeries are performed in the Texas Medical Center than anywhere else in the world.

According to a 2008 study, the Texas Medical Center generates $1.44 in government revenues for each $1 in pro-rated government costs. Every job in the Center creates 1.3 additional jobs in the community. One of every four hotel stays in the Houston area is related to health care and the Texas Medical Center. Memorial Hermann Life Flight operates around the clock and, since its inaugural flight, has flown more than 120,000 missions. When it opened in 1989, Harris Health System's Thomas Street Health Center was the first free-standing HIV/AIDS facility in the nation. Today, it is still one of America's largest HIV clinics.

Singapore, London, Boston, San Francisco—there is nothing quite like the Texas Medical Center. We have 21 renowned hospitals with seven acute care, six pediatric care and either specialty care facilities; three public health organizations; two universities; three medical schools; six nursing programs; two pharmacy schools; a dental school; eight academic and research institutions; and 13 support organizations.

Houston is an incredibly hospitable, vibrant, dynamic and business-friendly city that has so much going for it right now. The economy is great. It is by far the country's number one job creator. In talking about innovation, intellectual capital and information technology, besides the 54 member institutions of the Texas Medical Center, Houston is an economic powerhouse—with America's booming energy industry, 22 Fortune 500 companies, and let's not forget, the life-changing research performed every day at NASA.

JAMES T. WILLERSON, M.D.
James T. Willerson is the president and medical director of the Texas Heart Institute. He is also director of Cardiology Research, co-director of the Cullen Cardiovascular Research Laboratories, and co-director of Vulnerable Plaque Research at THI. Dr. Willerson was appointed president-elect of THI in 2004 and became president and medical director in 2008.

In Houston, the Texas Medical Center is the largest in the world, and there are four entities that rank in the top ten in the U.S.—M.D. Anderson Cancer Center, the Texas Heart Institute, Texas Children's Hospital and heart program, and the TIRR Memorial Hermann research and rehabilitation unit. Dallas is very competitive in all fields, including medicine, but there is no medical center in Dallas similar to the Texas Medical Center in Houston, either in size, diversity, national pre-eminence, number of patients treated or reputation.

I'm very proud of the openness of Houston people. It doesn't really matter who your father and mother were, or your name. What matters is what you want to do, whether you have something special to add, whether you will work to try to reach your goal. And if you are even a little bit successful, Houston's going to accept you and be supportive.

I have been a physician to many patients in Houston and Dallas, throughout Texas and across the world. I helped create an important bio-technology company called Volcano from the Texas Heart Institute. It has to do with catheters designed for detecting vulnerable plaques within coronary arteries that cause most heart attacks. My helping the University of Texas Medical School at Houston as the chairman of medicine and then later as president of the UT Health Science Center in Houston was a time in which we built eight new buildings, raised more than $1 billion, recruited many fine teachers and scientists, established the Institute of Molecular Medicine to identify and treat the genes and gene defects responsible for human disease.

I think these things have been useful contributions and they epitomize the positive sense that Houstonians in general have that nothing is impossible. My personal success can certainly be attributed to the opportunities I was given in both cities, but most recently in Houston, to contribute to the things I have described. In addition, the support of many people has given me the chance to do some useful things.

It is hard to pick only one moment in Houston's history because so many great things have happened in Houston over many years. The building of the Texas Medical Center would have to be among them. M.D. Anderson Cancer Center, the Texas Heart Institute, and Texas Children's Hospital are all sources of great pride to Houstonians. The Texas Medical Center is certainly one of the major contributions that Houston has made to the world. There is also the location of the manned space program here. The oil and gas industry, largely headquartered here, has also led the world.

Houston is a place where you are measured by your effort and your accomplishment, not by your family name. It is a place where challenge and success are encouraged, and even failure means you just have a new opportunity. Many places say they are cities of opportunity. Houston continually proves it. Houston and Dallas are both great cities. I have spent about an equal amount of time in each during my professional career. They are both cities of great generosity and great accomplishment. And both are very competitive. I have deep fondness for Dallas and people there, but Houston is a very, very special place.

DR. RONALD JONES

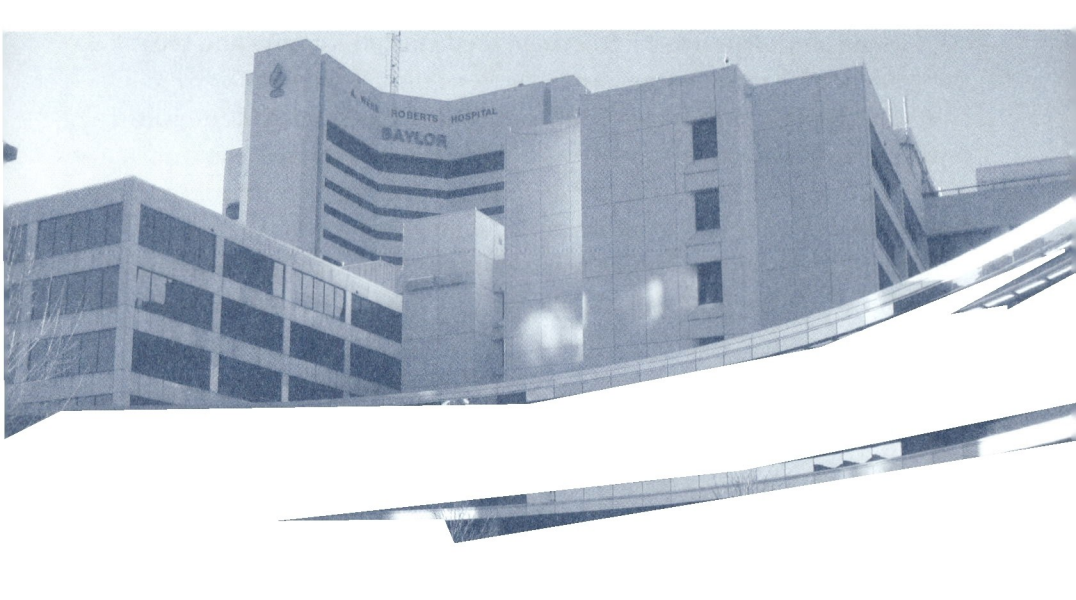

Dr. Ronald Jones, born in Arkansas and trained as a physician in Little Rock, Memphis, Los Angeles and Oklahoma City, and came to Dallas in 1960 for a residency in general surgery in 1960. In that capacity, he was waiting as President John F. Kennedy was rushed into Parkland Memorial Hospital on November 22, 1963, and then again two days when assassin Lee Harvey Oswald was shot by Jack Ruby. After years of service as part and then chairman of the University of Texas Southwestern Medical School, he moved in 1987 to chair the Baylor University Medical Center.

At Baylor, we're probably the largest general surgery program in a community-based hospital in the United States. And over at Parkland, with its connection to the University of Texas, they have the largest general surgery program in a university hospital in the United States. That means that in the entire country, both of the largest general surgery programs are right here in Dallas. That is certainly something we can be very proud of.

DALLAS: *Baylor University Medical Center*

05: MEDICINE

I came to Dallas from Oklahoma City in 1960, and what I saw then is still true now: almost anything you could ever wish for in the arts, entertainment or sports can be enjoyed right here. My late wife had graduated from Texas University for Women in Denton (now University of North Texas) so moving here was a nice homecoming for her. But first and foremost was my interest in becoming a surgeon. Then as now, if you want to become a surgeon, Dallas is probably the single best place to do it. Those two hospitals do amazing work training surgeons. The community knows this and supports them philanthropically.

Parkland was unusual when I arrived there in that its facilities were, for the most part, new and relatively up to date. The location of Harry Hines made it the third Parkland, and it had been built there less than ten years earlier. Though it was very much a community hospital, it had many of the same advantages of a private hospital. That quality certainly contributed to my growth as a surgeon, both while I was there and after my primary focus had moved to teaching at Southwestern. Today at Baylor, ours is a five-year program, as are most programs at the other 235 or so medical schools that offer such a thing. But whenever surveys are done, the number one preferred hospital in Dallas is usually Baylor. Plus, most of the surgeons in Dallas and the surrounding areas trained at either Baylor or Parkland. This expertise is a huge part of the city.

Back in 1969, Mayor Wes Wise launched the Greater Dallas League of Municipalities devoted to forming a long-range vision for North Texas, and one part of that was establishing an ambulance service. I became chairman of the committee that over the next two years established that service and got everybody comfortable with the way it worked. Before then, if you needed an ambulance around here, you got either a hearse from the funeral home or a station wagon. It wasn't easy, and we were voted down by the City Council the first time we asked them to fund the service. Even after Dallas came around, a lot of the surrounding communities still refused, claiming they weren't interested in giving money to help Dallas. When Dallas finally got an ambulance service in 1972, all the surrounding communities kept asking us why they hadn't been included.

Dallas has one of the best symphony orchestras in America,

playing both the classics and the pops, in a symphony hall designed by I.M. Pei. That's the branch of the arts I'm most involved in now, but there are other activities here as well. My wife and I took private dance lessons once a week for fifteen years, and we belonged to eight or nine dance clubs that held black-tie dances several times a year. Those events were always nice, but dancing is like playing piano—you never get where you want to be.

DR. HOWARD MOORE

A pioneer in the specialty of sports medicine, Dallas-born Howard Moore came to the focus logically enough—by playing football and running track at Tulane University. After early experiences in New Orleans and Seattle, Moore returned to his hometown and joined longtime associate J. Pat Evans at the Sports Medicine Clinic of North Texas in 1978. Since then, he has worked closely with the Dallas Cowboys, Dallas Mavericks and Dallas Sidekicks, as well as with area colleges and high schools.

When it comes to medicine in Dallas, it's not one-size-fits all any more. When I was growing up here, there were two maybe three medical centers: Parkland, Baylor and Methodist in Oak Cliff. Now there are many different types of hospitals, from small community facilities to big chains. I practice at Baylor because it's where I started and it's where I'm most comfortable.

I was fortunate, when I came through my training, that I was able to work alongside J. Pat Evans, who was pretty much the innovator of sports medicine. He stopped seeing general orthopedics patients and started focusing on athletes, becoming the team doctor for the Dallas Cowboys. And he invited me to practice with him, as long as I was willing to do nothing but sports medicine. I got in on the ground floor, before a lot of doctors even knew what sports medicine was. That was revolutionary. We even hired an athletic trainer from the Miami Dolphins. We lured him here to run our physical therapy clinic. It was a one-stop shop. The greatest form of flattery is to have somebody copy you, and shortly after we opened we had several competitors.

In some ways, the sub-specialties that have developed out of sports medicine do take away some of our business. But realistically, those doctors see things I don't see very often and therefore they are able to very cutting edge. In the old days, the orthopedic surgeon would probably do all of this. The athletes are much better off with all this specialization.

Over time, we developed a program to focus on schools. Part of our practice was to have an outreach to small towns with small high schools all across North Texas. Most didn't have a physician or even a nurse practitioner to evaluate the kids, so we tried to lift that level of care. We started a Saturday morning clinic, so that an athlete who was injured Thursday or Friday night could come in and we would evaluate him free of charge. We told them if they needed surgery, or else we sent a note back to the coach saying what kind of treatment the kid needed. We built a whole practice around that.

Dallas has provided a setting where we could expand our practice and do what we needed to do. In Chicago or New York, the medical community was very rigid and hard to break into. Dallas provided a platform. When I started, the medical community in Dallas was very collegial. Everybody worked together. Now it's kind of flip-flopped. All these hospitals have their own turf. The physicians have become pawns and aren't allowed to talk to each other. The hospitals have taken over. I've resisted that. I'm in a group of five surgeons, and we're associates rather than partners. I'm still independent, and I hope to retire that way.

DR. KENNETH COOPER

More than 40 years ago, Kenneth H. Cooper, MD, MPH, inspired millions to exercise for good health with the release of his first best-seller Aerobics. *Born in Oklahoma City in 1931, Cooper's father, a periodontist, instilled in him the desire to practice preventive medicine. Cooper received a bachelor of science and doctor of medicine at The University of Oklahoma, as well as a master of public health from Harvard.*

For decades, with doctors like Cooley and DeBakey, Houston was the medical capital of the world when it came to heart surgery and cancer treatment. That has continued, with the care in those areas second to none. But when it comes to preventative medicine, the area I've been blessed enough to work in creating Cooper Aerobics, it's said Dallas is the capital of the world. In those days, when I was first getting started right out of the Air Force, there was a saying around the medical profession: There's no profit in health. We've all learned the hard way that it's cheaper to keep people healthy than it is to cure them once they're sick. That message has been the story of my life, starting out in Dallas and now spreading the word to China, Switzerland and other countries all over the world.

I wrote my first book, *Aerobics*, back in 1968, and there have been eighteen other books since then. By 1970, when I came to Dallas and opened with two employees, I thought I'd have an overwhelming number of people trying to come to my clinic. That, it turned out, was not correct. I had to borrow $2,000 a month for two years to pay those employees. There were a lot of times I didn't think we were going to make it. It was tough, let me tell you. And for a lot of reasons, the traditional medical community in Dallas wasn't supportive at all. They called me a quack. They tried to run me out of town. They didn't understand what I was trying to do, and they definitely didn't like it. They told me I was going to kill people.

In retrospect, there were several good reasons I chose to locate in Dallas. I actually went down to Houston first, since I had so many good friends who were practicing medicine there. But the day I went there, it felt like a Turkish oven outside, and I said: Man, I don't want that. I also realized that, since I came from Oklahoma City and had spent years with the Air Force in San Antonio, that every time I wanted to go someplace, I had to go to Dallas to catch a plane. In terms of my plans, being in Dallas made a lot of sense to me.

Whenever I'm going overseas to speak, as I have in more than fifty countries, people hear I'm from Dallas and mention two names: J.R. Ewing and John F. Kennedy, neither of which say much about who we really are. Dallas is a very strong Christian community. We have a lot of great things going on in terms of the arts and culture, and we have a mayor who's making some wonderful changes. We have incredible philanthropy here too. The giving community in Dallas is second to none, whether you're talking about time, effort or money.

Today Cooper Aerobics has 750 employees in eleven divisions spread over thirty acres. We've published more than three hundred scientific papers about the value of preventative medicine, especially when it comes to cancer and heart disease. The importance of this message is why I left the Air Force even though I was climbing up the ladder in rank. I was successful, I realized, but I wasn't significant. I wasn't doing anything to help mankind. Now I think that's exactly what our work is doing.

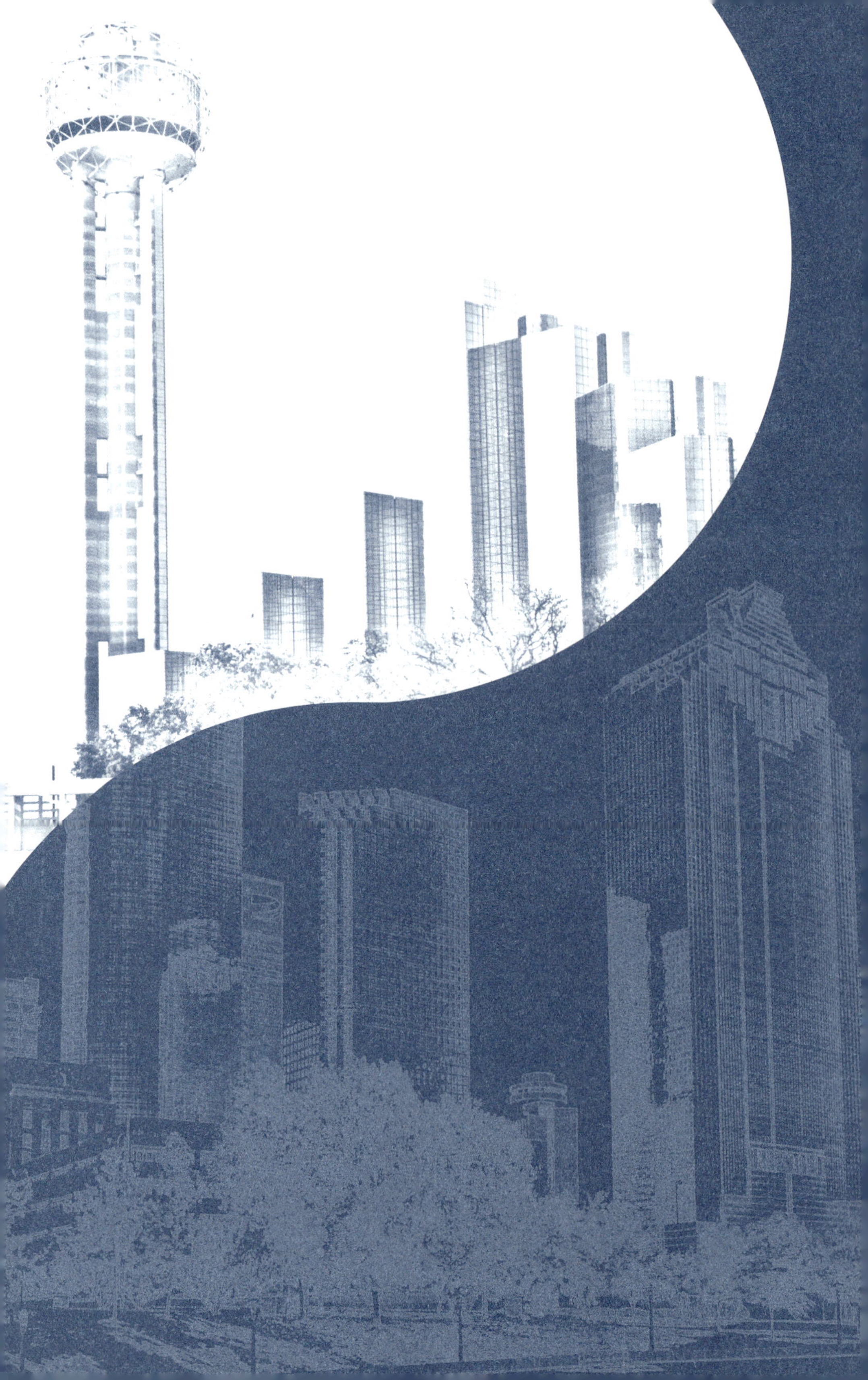

06

EDUCATION

Both Dallas and Houston are major metropolitan areas, and as such, they've been beset by the same financial and cultural pressures on their education systems that virtually all similar cities have suffered. Most importantly, the chasm between the haves and have-nots has grown in terms of public schools, with both the quality of facilities and the likelihood of success diminishing in many areas year after year. Solutions have been suggested, and, as far back the 1960s, some have been implemented.

One solution for parents, of course, has been to send children to private schools. Whether those are faith-based or simply private, that is an avenue unavailable to most of the population. Another is home schooling, which certainly can point to many adherents in Texas for any number of reasons, whatever its pros and cons. Still, most educators (and nearly all business leaders) believe a viable, success-producing public school system is essential. Out of this belief have come reform movements, whether focusing on the creation of charter schools, producing more trained and motivated teachers, seeking more accurate assessment of results and–this being Texas–debating fine points of curriculum.

Many people in both Dallas and Houston have big ideas for improving public schools, some primarily religious, some mostly political and some a mixture of the two. Public schools matter, and Texans have never backed away from the challenge of trying to make things that *matter* better.

MIKE MILES

Mike Miles became the 25th superintendent of the Dallas Independent School District in 2012. During his first two years on the job, Miles worked with the Dallas ISD Board of Trustees to approve new evaluation systems for both principals and teachers tied to student performance. The new teacher evaluation system, which provides regular feedback and compensates educators based on effectiveness, is believed to be at the forefront of pay for performance models among school districts throughout the country. Miles is a former U.S. Diplomat, Army Ranger, teacher, middle school principal and previously served as the superintendent of Harrison District 2 in Colorado Springs.

Dallas is an exceptional place to live, a place where residents expect a public school system that reaches all students to help them succeed. As educators, we have a tremendous responsibility to prepare students for a future that looks very different from yesterday and includes jobs that haven't even been imagined yet. That means we have

DALLAS: *Southern Methodist University*

to think of innovative ways to reach students, provide a high quality education, and meet the needs of tomorrows workforce.

This is a big task. One that Dallas citizens, with high expectations for themselves, their children and their city, is ready to tackle. During the past two years the district has taken bold steps to move toward academic achievement, and we are seeing gains. Thanks to the dedication of our teachers and staff, and the hard work they've collectively put in, our four-year graduation rate increased each of the last five years and the percentage of students dropping out of high school dropped each of those years. Our students have also shown progress on the STAAR and EOC (End of Course) exams.

Our work is guided by our Destination 2020, our strategic plan designed to establish an educational system that focuses on continuous improvement, excellence, and accountability. The plan serves as a blueprint for transforming our schools and we know that principals and teachers are key to our efforts. Dallas ISD has placed great emphasis on developing principals as highly effective instructional leaders and building support systems for teachers that in turn rewards excellence in the classroom.

The adoptions of a new principal evaluation system and the Teacher Excellence Initiative (TEI) have been important steps in our work. These systems are tied to student performance and are designed to strengthen the quality of instruction as well as create a culture of effective instructional feedback. Under the rigorous TEI system teachers have the opportunity to increase their annual compensation faster than under a traditional pay model.

In addition to the emphasis we have placed on what is happening inside the classroom, we are expanding access to quality pre-Kindergarten instruction to include more students. We will also add more school choice options for students during the next six years, including schools that offer personalized learning, which is a "one-size fits one" approach to meeting students' academic needs with instruction they need when they need it.

Dallas ISD is thinking differently and acting courageously. We are committed to preparing all students for college and the workforce. To learn more about our work visit DallasISD.org.

ALEXANDRA HALES

Alex Hales is Executive Director of Teach For America's Dallas-Fort Worth region. She joined the South Louisiana Teach For America corps as a first grade teacher in 2007, where she was named District Teacher of the Year for East Feliciana Parish. Two years later, Alex was a key leader in opening the Teach For America charter region in North Texas, where she first served as a manager of teacher leadership development and now leads the region, currently in its 6th year in Dallas-Fort Worth.

As a large urban area, Dallas faces many of the challenges to public education that other major cities do. Dallas has seen an ever-growing divide of educational access between lower income students and their wealthier peers over the last 25 years. In the Dallas Independent School District, where approximately 90% of the student population is considered economically disadvantaged, just 13% of students are prepared for college. In stark contrast, in nearby Highland Park, none of the school system's 6,000 students qualify for free or reduced lunch and 98% go on to attend a four year university.

Since our launch in Dallas-Fort Worth in 2009, Teach For America has worked to build strong relationships in the education community and deepen our impact over time. In that time, our presence in the region has more than quadrupled in size. Our corps of more than 450 teachers impacts approximately 36,000 students. Community leaders and stakeholders, from superintendents to teachers to parents of students that we teach, business owners, and religious leaders, value the source of strong teachers we provide. The DFW community is committed to improving public education in Dallas, and Teach For America is part of the effort to reach that goal, through expanding our teacher training to all teachers, and developing an alumni network dedicated to teaching, administration, and education nonprofits and advocacy organizations.

Heading into our sixth year, we've developed strong partnerships that have enabled us to make an even greater impact in the Dallas-Fort Worth region beyond training and supporting great teachers in classrooms. Through a program called the Middle School Partnership Plan, Teach For America–Dallas-Fort Worth partnered with two local middle schools to provide high-quality professional development through real-time coaching, content training and improved instructional feedback cycles for all teachers at these schools. The success of the Middle School Partnership Plan has led to an expansion in several other DFW middle schools.

Last year, we launched the Balanced Literacy Initiative in partnership with Commit! (a coalition supporting Dallas County public schools) in prioritized elementary schools in the Molina High School feeder pattern and the South Oak Cliff area. This initiative provides balanced literacy training, a method of teaching, reading, writing, speaking, listening and viewing for Dallas ISD instructional coaches to work with teachers at these schools to ultimately increase student learning and success in the classroom.

DFW is well positioned for comprehensive changes in public education that ensure every child growing up in the region has the opportunity to get a great education. The Metroplex has city and school leaders dedicated to improving schools, a strong nonprofit network providing innovative support and programs for students, and a deep understanding of what it's going to take to get improve the quality of education every child has the opportunity to receive. The community believes the commitment, leadership and enthusiasm possessed by Teach For America corps members and alumni can play a big part in fueling that movement. Today, we see TFA alums continuing to make a huge impact in DFW classrooms, leading schools as principals, and steering education nonprofits such as The Teaching Trust and Education Opens Doors.

Two things going on in Dallas-Fort Worth right now give me the greatest hope. One is the recognition that there is a lot that needs to be done to make sure every child in Dallas and Fort Worth is getting a great education. The other is the community-wide partnership among committed individuals and organizations to increase education opportunities for DFW students.

GERALDINE "TINCY" MILLER

Tincy Miller is a native of Dallas. She married a fellow Dallasite, the late Vance C. Miller, and helped him grow his family's business, Henry S. Miller, into the largest commercial real estate company in Texas. She has been active as a patron of the arts and a champion of education, serving on the state Board of Education for 27 years and returning to it in 2012.

I'd like to see teachers in our public schools be as highly qualified as those in our charter schools, and that requires the parents and guardians to be involved. We cannot mandate a parent to be involved in a child's education—I wish we could—but all we can do is encourage. I believe that every child should read, since reading is the basis of everything. I believe that all kids should learn and learn well. I believe that our textbooks should be accurate. But we have to stay on top of it.

In the Constitution of 1875, our pioneers took oil and gas money and created the State Board of Education. Now that's a $29-$30 billion fund, generating $700 million to $800 million a year to supply free textbooks for every child in public school in Texas. In my tenure, I've found that every two years the Legislature tries to raid this fund, which is ranked right under Harvard as the best performing education endowment in the nation. They can't seem to understand why they're not overseeing it. But our pioneers were wise enough to not let that happen.

I am proud of Dallas because it is a can-do city, friendly and open, with a small town feeling yet a keen sense of sophistication. My personal success comes from my many friends and family and colleagues in Dallas, and from the great opportunities our city has to offer. Ours is a city that attracts economic growth and philanthropy. Vance and I married after we both graduated from SMU, and we shared his incredible experience in the Air Force and then came back to Dallas. Vance and I were married 56 years and raised four children (all graduates of SMU), and eight grandchildren.

My contribution to the city is my involvement in helping underprivileged children become successful and graduating from high school. On the Board of Education, I facilitated the first Dyslexia

Law in Texas and in the nation, teaching children identified with dyslexia to read, write and spell, and also implemented the first phonics-based curriculum standards in the Texas public schools. Both of those programs are still going strong.

It is said that a city is not great without the arts. Dallas has achieved that goal with the recent completion of the Performing Arts Center. One of my contributions was inaugurating the Dallas Symphony Orchestra Debutante Presentation in 1986-1987 that has since grown to netting $400,000 to $500,000 each year, with at least 40 young college-age ladies making their bow escorted by the young men of the Honor Guard. Another joy over the years has been helping my mother-in-law, Juanita Miller, start and grow the Dallas Opera, the Symphony and the Theater Center. We are especially proud today of the new Perot Museum of Natural History, the Winspear Opera House, the Meyerson Symphony Center and the Wyly Theatre.

Defining moments in Dallas can be as exciting as the Dallas Cowboys getting their beginning with Clint Murchison or as sad as the day President Kennedy was shot. We watched with pride as the Cowboys won all those Super Bowls, and our city pulled together to create The Sixth Floor Museum commemorating that sad day half a century ago. Dallas rose from the ashes of that terrible day. We used that tragedy to become better.

LUIS ELIZONDO-THOMSON

San Antonio-born Luis Elizondo-Thomson joined the Teach for America team in 2013 as Houston executive director, leading one of Teach for America's original regions. His previous experience includes five years as an investment banker specializing in infrastructure finance and several years working in local and national politics.

I love the diversity of this city. Houston is not the kind of place that cares about your pedigree. The only questions are: are you smart, are you hard-working, and are you willing to give back to the city. If you can say yes to those three questions, you'll be at home in Houston. Having been active here for more than twenty years, we're now seeing people who came to teach here through Teach For America as 22 and 23 year olds in 1995 have now become local leaders in education. And their students are graduating from college and joining the Teach For America-Houston teaching corps to lead the classrooms where they once studied. We're fortunate to work with so

HOUSTON: *Rice University*

many other organizations across the city who are working towards the same goal of expanding educational opportunity for all Houston kids—and on top of that many of our alumni are now leading those organizations.

Since 1991, nearly 2,000 Teach For America corps members have taught in Houston's low-income schools, reaching nearly 200,000 students collectively and becoming some of our city's most prominent education leaders. Now nearly 450 corps members are teaching 40,000 students across Houston. An additional 1,000 Teach For America alumni living in Houston continue working inside and outside the field of education to bring the fundamental changes necessary to ensure educational excellence and equity. With 37 alumni school and district leaders, the creation of two charter school systems and an establishment of several non-profit organizations targeting educational inequity, Teach For America is living out its mission in Houston.

What we're trying to do is bring about an immediate, short-term impact in the classrooms in lower-income neighborhoods while also, in the long-term, strengthening the education system. When Teach For America began, our we focused on recruiting diverse campus leaders from the top-tier universities all across the country, and those people are the ones now becoming our leaders here. More recently, we've expanded our focus seen a significant up-tick in the number of successful professionals leaving other sectors to teach with us to do something where they could make a huge impact.

I don't think it's an accident that Teach For America came to Houston more than twenty years ago and has been growing and evolving ever since. Houston is the kind of city that has a deep and rich entrepreneurial spirit. If you can dream it, you can do it in a city like Houston. My greatest hope, and also the greatest challenge we have, is that Houston has all the resources it needs to make transformational change in the education space. Houston has the wealth capacity, and we have an incredible history of philanthropy. We now have nearly every major education organization operating here. Because of our diversity, whatever we figure out here can be modeled and replicated throughout the country. There are best practices we can learn here that are meaningful for others.

The challenge is that we aren't working together enough to really collaborate in a sophisticated way. As soon as we realize that the future will require collaboration rather than competition, we'll be ready to turn the corner in education. We're going to have to co-produce the success.

RENU KHATOR

Renu Khator is the 8th chancellor of the University of Houston System and the 13th president of the University of Houston. She is the first foreign-born president of the university, and the second woman to hold the position. Khator is also the first Indian-American to lead a major research university in the United States.

I thank God every day for making me a University of Houston Cougar. Since I became president of UH in 2008, I've learned many things about the city whose name our university shares. I know which freeways can get crowded. Where to buy good rodeo clothes and where to find high fashion. What the best dishes are at my favorite restaurants. How to pronounce "San Felipe" like a Houstonian. And I learned it's not the heat, it's the humidity. But the most important thing I've learned is Houston truly appreciates the importance of higher education. We have enjoyed unprecedented levels of support from civic and business leaders, generous financial backing from donors and continuing community enthusiasm for our efforts to transform UH into a nationally competitive public research university. I think Houston's encouragement and assistance in UH achieving Tier One status was an act of enlightened self-interest. A great community needs a great public university.

Certainly, our community is great for a number of reasons—not the least of which is Houston's admirable diversity. Demographers point to Houston as a model for the city of the future. UH reflects that same quality—we are the second most diverse research university in America, according to the *U.S. News & World Report* rankings. Of course, Houston is also very special because of its entrepreneurial spirit. Houston really is place where people are judged by the content of their character and what they try to accomplish.

In that regard, I'm proud to say UH has played a significant role. When I first arrived, I asked the campus community and the people of Houston what they wanted me to accomplish. Basically, I was tasked with elevating UH into the top tier of schools and transforming it into a nationally recognized research university. All right, I said, but that's a real challenge, and it could take seven or eight years. Maybe a decade. As it turned out, we earned Tier One status in four years—half the time. Obviously, I'm delighted about Houston getting the kind of first-rate public university it needs, but it was really was a team effort, with all of us, the university and the city, pulling together to make it happen.

Although Houston has been "my" city for a relatively short period, I have been tremendously impressed by its continuing economic success. That is a defining characteristic. Looking at Houston across its history, I would single out the Allen Brothers deciding to establish this city in the first place. There were many reasons not to, but the brothers were bold and committed—like Houston itself. Other defining moments? "Houston" being the first word spoken from the Moon. College sports fans might suggest the Game of the Century, when UH's basketball team beat undefeated UCLA in the Astrodome in 1968. That was the first NCAA regular season game broadcast nationwide in prime time—and the beginning of "March Madness." No doubt, the invention of air conditioning was a crucial development for Houston. Speaking of which—did you know UH had the *first* air-conditioned college building in the world?

Finally, the notable diversity we see in the population is also reflected in the culture and lifestyle of the city. We have the full range of high-brow performances and fine arts—Houston has more theater seats than any other city in the country besides New York—along with rodeo, rock concerts, chili cook-offs, drag races and marathons. We have professional sports teams to admire and college teams to root for (Go, Coogs!), including a brand-new 40,000 seat football stadium here at UH. We enjoy a dazzling array of restaurants, with just about every cuisine in the world available somewhere around town. For many, it's a high-low lifestyle, watching soccer one weekend and listening to Mahler the next. We Houstonians like ourselves, and we love our city.

BARBARA CARGILL

A native of Memphis, Barbara Cargill won election to the Texas State Board of Education from a district that now includes 20% of Harris County plus all or part of eight others. Still a teacher at heart, she was appointed to back-to-back terms as board chairman by Governor Rick Perry, winning approval by a two-thirds vote of the state Senate.

I know Houston is a welcoming city because it was welcoming to me when I was a stranger. The people of Houston are wonderful. Serving on the Board of Education is a labor of love and a passion and a calling. Today, with the changing dynamics of Texas and so many different varieties of students, we simply have to teach our students as individuals. We want them to get a good education, of course, but it is absolutely critical that our public schools meet the needs of each individual child. For all the great work that our private schools do, I like to say that I'm the A-number-1 cheerleader for public schools.

As parents, our children always come first. I have yet to meet a parent whose child doesn't, and I'm talking to parents all the time. When people move to Texas with children, checking out the public schools is one of their very first priorities. And in the community itself, having a good public school system matters so much. I am always encouraging local businesses to get involved with their community school system. I think it's a great concept when parents and local businesses take ownership of their schools and support their kids. You can't get a better combination than that.

Math, science and technology form the direction that our nation and our world are traveling for the foreseeable future. I'm a big proponent of the well-rounded education. You have to have good skills in reading to learn math and science, and our Founding Fathers wanted us to always keep passing history down as well. But in recent years, especially in math and science, we've been working closely with businesses and with the colleges that continue educating our students, all to make sure the skills we teach are what they need in the years ahead. In a way that wasn't always the case, we are working closely with the Texas Higher Education Coordinating Board. And we are working with the Texas Workforce Commission, matching up the expectation of job skills for specific jobs in Texas. Schools can drop in the skills the Workforce Commission provides and be better able to craft their courses.

One of our main duties on the board is writing and implementing curriculum standards. The board has worked earnestly to make these standards very strong, very applicable, very rigorous and very clear. If we believe in our students and believe in our teachers, then we're off to a great start.

As a teacher and as a mother of three boys, one of the things I'm proudest of is starting a summer science program in the Woodlands for three-and-a-half-year-olds to fourth graders. My own boys inspired it all when they were really small, and I was impressed with what little sponges kids that age are. We just celebrated our 20th anniversary. In our program, they're learning what metamorphosis is. They're learning what a habitat is. We've raised the bar very high with these kids. Teaching is a gift, and I feel I have to put the gift to use.

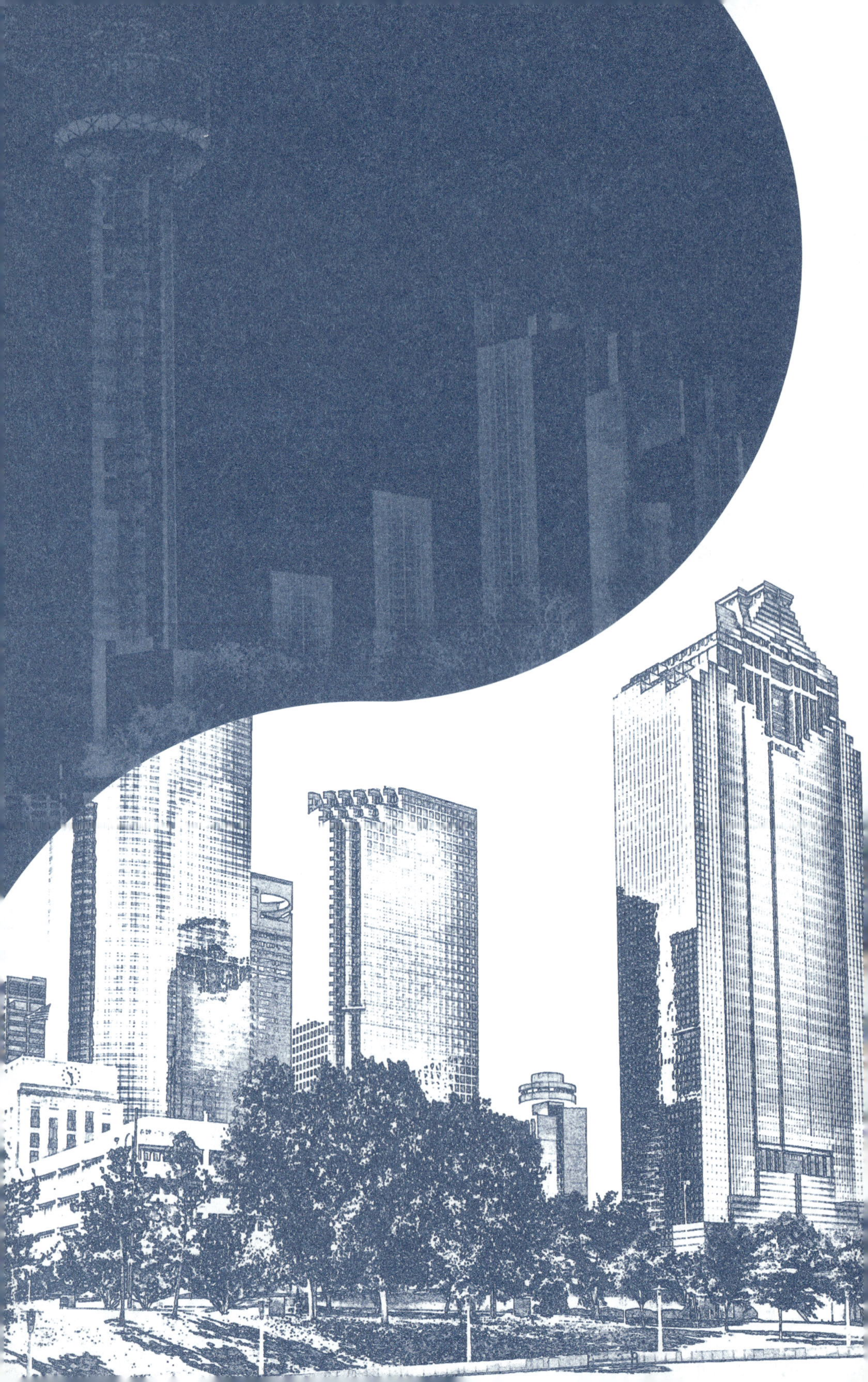

07

ARCHITECTURE

Dallas and Houston are cities in a hurry. And from an architectural standpoint, that's usually bad news. They're in a hurry to create, to launch, to innovate, and definitely in a hurry to get rich. That most often adds up to a near-complete lack of interest in preserving the past and, in some quarters, a dazzling lack of interest in designing the future. At our Texas worst, buildings seem disposable tools used for the presumed greater good and then simply discarded. Many parts of that traditional description are changing, however.

Most dramatically, the leaderships of both cities are finally recognizing landmarks more readily today than they ever did in the past, arguably a function of moving away from a frontier-survival mentality toward the kind of grace and tradition that define older cities like Boston. Texans are coming to realize that we can borrow the best aspects of older cities without succumbing to what we sometimes judge as their lack of innovation, their lack of drive. As both Dallas and Houston came into their own architecturally in the 20th century (with only a handful of relics from the 19th), they naturally display the host of styles popular during the time, such as Art Deco. A certain sifting has taken place to be sure, with surprising nostalgia gathering around buildings that few even noticed in decades past.

In addition, business leaders building their fortunes in Dallas and Houston have realized they are building their legacies as well. Few things are more permanent than a major edifice, whether it's a private space for doing business or a public space for storing books, hosting performances, healing the sick or enjoying sports. All these types of buildings have, with the arrival of the 21st century, become not only functions but forms we can view with civic pride.

07: ARCHITECTURE

COLE SMITH
Cole Smith, a partner at Smith, Ekblad & Associates, is one of the most prominent and important architects in Dallas. He has faithfully recreated designs from Europe and secured craftsmen and tradesmen from around the world to help him in this mission.

An important early event in my professional life was doing a small apartment building for Mr. H.L. Hunt and asking him what kind of contract we should make. He said, "Son, we've already done that when we shook hands after you came in." When I asked him about the fee, he looked me in the eye and said very seriously, "You will be fair." He was, and I was, and that is mostly the way I have conducted business for 63 years. When I came to Dallas from Kansas in 1950, this city was full of opportunity and very welcoming to a young architect and his new wife. To me, Dallas has always represented friendliness, opportunity and a wonderful place to work.

As an architect, I'd say Dallas's growth has made my career possible. The level of elegance and quality that many people have wanted

DALLAS: *Frank Lloyd Wright's Kalita Humphreys Theater*

has enabled me to create homes, offices, churches and many other buildings that give me pride, and I hope give my clients ongoing pleasure. I am lucky to still be working and creating new homes and other buildings in my eighth decade, all due to the business opportunities and great clients in Dallas. Although I have done work over the U.S. and in several other countries, my main practice has always been in and around Dallas.

The Dallas lifestyle is many-faceted. It depends on your age, finances and location, but there are limitless opportunities in every direction. According to the younger set, there is a lively club and live music world out there. There are almost too many restaurants to count, with every type of cuisine. According to my wife, and judging by the size of her closet, the shopping opportunities are abundant. There are churches everywhere, from small struggling ones to mega worship centers. If your wish is to practice your faith, whether Baptist or Buddhist, there are plenty of churches, synagogues and folks waiting to welcome you. The arts seem to be especially blossoming. Music is one of my great loves, and the Dallas Opera, Dallas Symphony, the Bach Society and many other special groups provide more opportunities than we can keep up with.

And of course, a main part of the Dallas lifestyle is to work hard and play hard—and enjoy life at home with friends as often as possible, usually with one eye on the steaks cooking on the grill and the other eye on the Cowboys or Mavericks or whatever game is playing at the time.

While Dallas is generally conservative financially, I have seen more and more evidence of a growing concern for the environment and for the less fortunate among the people I know. More awareness of architecture and art is everywhere, and that makes me especially happy. The world's natural beauty must be conserved, and everything that is built needs to enhance the world rather than degrade it. The more people that appreciate beauty and beautiful things, the better.

In over 60 years in Dallas, I don't think I've ever heard a single person say anything particularly negative about Houston, except for its climate. More often than not, people here have relatives or friends there. I personally like the weather in Dallas better because it's drier and cooler. But Houston is a terrific, exciting place. Their museums, medical centers and resources are top-notch, and their people couldn't be finer. Texas is lucky to have both of these cities.

GREG BROWN

Greg Brown serves as program director at the Dallas Center for Architecture. The organization was founded by the American Institute of Architects Dallas in 2008 to encourage the conversation about why architecture matters through its public programs, exhibits, scholarships and tours.

Dallas has always had a "can-do" spirit that permeates everything we do. Certainly, that has led to business successes, but it has also led to some real architectural triumphs as well. We battled other Texas cities to get the Texas Centennial Exposition in 1936 and now have the finest collection of Art Deco exposition buildings in the world. The economic boom of the 1980s led to developers hiring some of the best architects in Dallas and across the world to create a skyline of post-Modern buildings that remains iconic. And more recently, we closed another chapter in a 30-year effort to create the largest urban arts district in the country. It is filled with fine buildings, both historic and contemporary, by architects from here at home and around the world, including four Pritzker Architecture Prize laureates.

In recent years, Dallas has become diverse in so many ways. There are wonderful neighborhoods full of ethnic cuisines and culture, dive bars and white-glove restaurants, Big Business and entrepreneurs. They all fit in in Big D. Dallas is indeed aspirational because we are never satisfied with the status quo. Everything must be getting better all the time. Our transportation systems, our neighborhoods, our food, our parks—all come from that desire to be the best we can be.

Dallas has gone through several periods of prolific and great architecture. The 1920s and 1930s brought us icons as varied as the Magnolia Building, the Titche-Goettinger Building and the original home of Republic Bank. The year 1931 brought three of downtown's best Art Deco buildings by architects Mark Lemmon and the firm Lang & Witchell. Residential architecture was also important during this period with stately homes going up in the Swiss

Avenue neighborhood as well as the "suburbs" of University Park and Highland Park. A culmination of that period was the Art Deco masterpiece at Fair Park that was created by George Dahl and his team for the Texas Centennial Exposition.

There was also a post-World War II boom that brought about the aluminum-clad Republic National Bank and office buildings like the Meadows Building outside the central business district. Again, residential architecture is important with architects like Howard Meyer, O'Neil Ford and others adapting mid-century style for Dallas taste and materials.

With the construction of Reunion Tower and the Hyatt Regency in 1978, downtown Dallas saw a high-rise building boom as important post-Modernists like Philip Johnson, I.M. Pei and Richard Keating constructed one-of-a-kind office buildings that make up our unique downtown look. With the economic collapse of the 1980s, that skyline was frozen for two decades. We seem to be in another boom of sorts, but the accomplishments are not just buildings. Klyde Warren Park and the Calatrava-designed Margaret Hunt Hill Bridge join the buildings completing the Dallas Arts District and Thom Mayne's Perot Museum to signal a new chapter. And downtown is building again too—new residential and office towers as well as older buildings being transformed for new purposes.

Beauty is always in the eye of the beholder, but I like to show visitors the breadth and variety of our architecture. You should see Swiss Avenue for a snapshot of the residences of wealthy and powerful Dallasites in the 1920s and beyond. An icon that stands out to me on our skyline is Fountain Place, not only for its Pei Cobb Freed-designed tower but also its incredible Dan Kiley water garden. Main Street Garden offers a vantage point of a timeline of Dallas' architectural history—from the Beaux Arts Municipal Building to Conrad Hilton's first high-rise hotel and the later 1950s Statler Hilton.

Recent buildings that create discussion (whether you love them or hate them) are the Wyly Theater of the AT&T Performing Arts Center and the Perot Museum of Nature and Science. And I always want folks to see Fair Park, the largest collection of Art Deco exhibition buildings anywhere—a real jewel that is being steadily restored by the city to its original glory.

07: ARCHITECTURE

MARK LAMSTER

Mark Lamster is the architecture critic of The Dallas Morning News *and a professor in the architecture school at the University of Texas at Arlington. He is presently at work on a biography of the late architect Philip Johnson.*

Dallas has a great deal of wonderful architecture, but it has a reputation, not undeserved, for ostentation, for tearing things down and for sacrificing itself to the automotive gods—and that overshadows much of the discussion about the city.

Dallas is constantly reinventing itself. If there is one architect who defines Dallas it is probably George Dahl, who began working in the early 20th century in the Beaux Arts tradition, was design director of Fair Park, and wound up designing in the modern idiom, including the very modern Gold Crest apartment building, in which he himself lived. I think everyone takes the city for granted, and because we drive so much generally fail to stop and notice what's here.

Here are the 10 Dallas buildings I think are most worth noticing:

1. Bryan Cabin: Dallas begins with this simple house built in the mid-19th century, and it remains a prominent, if not entirely authentic, presence in the heart of downtown. For both better and worse, it established the residential paradigm of this city: the single-family detached house. A walk up to the Arts District will bring you to the Belo Mansion, the Ross Avenue home of *The Dallas Morning News* founder A. H. Belo, one of its many more opulent progenies.
2. Old Red (1892): The powerful, Richardsonian romanesque red-brick courthouse gives a solidity to a downtown skyline that often seems as ephemeral as a balloon. That it remains is a testament to the Dallas preservation movement, which celebrates its 40th anniversary this year.
3. Texas School Book Depository (1901): This handsome commercial structure, one of a handful remaining from an era when downtown Dallas was a bustling district of warehouses and light manufacturing, unwittingly became a defining work of architecture, one of the very few buildings in this city

almost every American of a certain age can name.
4. Adolphus Hotel (1912): The great Dowager of Downtown was the city's first true skyscraper, a 20-story chateaux-style tower of French-fried prairie opulence, if not ostentation. It was built by St. Louis beer baron Adolphus Busch, whose name it carries. Busch also financed the gothic-revival Kirby Building, around the corner, a lynchpin in the conversion of downtown into a mixed-use neighborhood of commercial and residential properties.
5. Knights of Pythias Temple (1916): The Deep Ellum landmark was built by an African-American architect, William Sidney Pittman, for an African-American clientele. It might no longer be the hub of a vibrant community, as it was in its heyday, but it remains a potent and distinguished symbol.
6. Hall of State, Fair Park (1936): The most regal of all the buildings of Fair Park, a joint production in the modern-classical style of the Depression years. The Centennial Exhibition, for which it was the centerpiece, established Dallas at the very top of the Texas urban hierarchy.
7. NorthPark Center (1965): In the 1960s, Dallas abandoned its center for the suburbs, and no building better epitomized that move than this handsome, modern shopping mall, with its gracious, light-filled design and sculpture program administered by its developer, Raymond Nasher.
8. Dallas City Hall (1978): Love it or hate it, I.M. Pei's City Hall building is inescapable, a monumental and imposing vision of civic governance. If the outside is obdurate—and removed from the city it would regulate—the interior is limpid and open.
9. Reunion Tower/Hyatt Regency Dallas at Reunion hotel (1978): The lollipop tower and gridded glass hotel are a skyline unto themselves, one that defines the western boundary of downtown. Scaleless and ephemeral, they shimmer from a distance, reinforcing the city's image as a space of endless possibility.
10. Fountain Place (1986): The shape-shifting prism—it's different from every angle—was designed by Harry Weese, the partner of I.M. Pei, and is without question the most handsome of

Dallas' skyscrapers. Its pointed top makes it an easy icon for the city. The fountained plaza at its base, designed by the modernist legend Dan Kiley, is among downtown's most rewarding public spaces.

HOUSTON: *The Menil Collection*

STEPHEN FOX
Stephen Fox is an architectural historian and a Fellow of the Anchorage Foundation of Texas. He is the author of the AIA Houston Architectural Guide *(2012) and a contributor to* The Buildings of Texas: Central, South, and Gulf Coast, *edited by Gerald Moorhead (2013).*

Houston is notorious for its lack of zoning, urban sprawl and visual squalor. Yet extreme aversion to the basic mechanics of American city planning and middle-class notions of tidiness has not resulted in a disdain for architecture. The city has supported approximately seven generations of talented local architects. The immense live oak trees that canopy the coastal plain imbue Houston with dignity and a sense of cultural specificity that the built environment frequently fails to provide.

In terms of architecture and landscape design, Houston's defining moments include the decision of Edgar Odell Lovett, the first president of what is now Rice University, to commission the Boston architect Ralph Adams Cram to plan Rice's campus and design its first buildings in 1909; the insistence of J. S. Cullinan, founder of the Texas Company, that the City of Houston retain the St. Louis landscape architect George E. Kessler to plan Hermann Park and the new Main Boulevard in 1914; the abiding interest that the lawyer Will C. Hogg took in planning for Houston's growth in the 1920s, to the extent that he and his family acquired the property for Memorial Park in 1924 and developed the garden suburban community of River Oaks beginning in 1925; the determination of Hogg's sister and collaborator, Ima Hogg, to formulate an architecture and landscape architecture specifically for Houston, which she did with the architect John F. Staub and the landscape architects Ruth London and C. C. Fleming in the 1920s and 30s.

There's also the courage of the Parisian émigrés Dominique and John de Menil in commissioning the New York architect Philip Johnson to design their house in 1948 and then recommending him for additional commissions as well as supporting such talented local architects as Howard Barnstone and Eugene Aubry, who launched the Tin House movement with their design of the Art Barn for the Menils in 1969; the resolution of J. S. Cullinan's daughter, Nina Cullinan, in specifying that the Museum of Fine Arts retain an outstanding architect to design the addition whose construction she underwrote, which led the museum to retain Ludwig Mies van der Rohe in 1954; the clarity with which Gerald D. Hines understood by the late 1960s that hiring the best architects in the U. S. would give his Houston real estate investment projects the competitive edge they needed to excel in the marketplace, which led him to build Philip Johnson and John Burgee's Pennzoil Place of 1976, a building that changed the course of skyscraper design worldwide.

There was the founding of the Rice Design Alliance in 1973 by David A. Crane, dean of Rice University's School of Architecture, as a public forum for architectural culture; Dominique de Menil's selection of Renzo Piano in 1981 to design a museum building for the collection she and her husband acquired; the artist Rick Lowe's confidence in 1994 that there was a future for 22 vacant and dilapidated rental cottages in the low-income, center-city, African American neighborhood of Third Ward, which led him and his associates to start the art installation, social services, historic preservation, and community reinvestment non-profit, Project Row Houses; the civic commitment of the founders of the Hermann Park Conservancy, who in 1995 retained the Philadelphia landscape architect Laurie Olin to plan for the restoration and rehabilitation of the exhausted park, and then methodically carried through, step by step, on Olin's proposals; and the perseverance of the art dealer Hiram Butler, who in 1999 persuaded Houston's Quaker meeting, the Live Oak Friends, Houston architect Leslie Elkins, and artist James Turrell to collaborate on building a Quaker meeting house containing one of Turrell's distinctive Skyspaces (2001).

These defining moments of the 20th century accomplished a major goal of defining moments: to inspire more. In their new building projects, Rice University, the Museum of Fine Arts, and the Menil Collection perpetuate the distinguished patronage of architecture and landscape architecture associated with past generations. And they encourage other local institutions, such as the Asia Society Texas Center, to act boldly in constructing exceptional architecture. Houston's collective aspirations are conventional and business oriented. It is the aspirations of individual Houstonians that lead to great things in terms of architecture.

BARRY MOORE

Houston-born architect Barry Moore has been working in the city since 1967. He is currently a senior associate at Gensler, one of the largest architecture firms in the country. The company, founded in San Francisco, opened its first branch office in Houston 42 years ago. Much of Moore's work has been focused on education and cultural venues.

Since 1836 Houston has been a port city and has become the most multi-cultural city in America. I am proud that it is an open city, open to newcomers—socially, culturally, and economically. It's not "who do you know," it's "what can you do?" It is a city with an entrepreneurial population.

For a huge, industrial city that's perceived as blue collar, Houston has an unbelievably generous and philanthropic population. As a result, we are one of three cities in the U.S. with a thriving opera company, symphony orchestra, ballet company, respected theater rep company, major museum of fine arts, one of the largest museums of natural science, and dozens of respected professional theater companies and private art galleries. We are in a league with New York and Los Angeles.

The planning and development in Houston is accomplished from the bottom up, not the top down, instigated by our private and non-profit sector rather than the public, often through the mechanisms of tax increment reinvestment zones, property deed restrictions, and the phenomenon of people just going out and doing something and then getting it embraced by the community. The result has given us the phenomenal development of the Galleria area, the restoration of The Orange Show and the Beer Can House, the celebration of the McKee Street Bridge as an engineering icon, and most recently, the Deer Park Native Prairie on the Houston Ship Channel.

My contributions, by virtue of my profession of architecture, are modest. I taught University of Houston graduate architecture students for 24 years, and made it a mission to stress the historic richness of the city and how as architects we have a role to protect and celebrate our many built treasures. My proudest achievement was leading our firm's team in the restoration of the 1926 Julia Ideson Library—one of the great historic buildings of Texas.

The foundation of my personal success is my education at Rice University, and as an educator at the University of Houston. My continuing involvement with the success of this city is realized through contributions to Rice Design Alliance's *Cite Magazine* and the Architecture Center Houston exhibition gallery.

Houston was founded on outrageous aspirations when it was selected as the Capitol of the Republic of Texas in 1836. It was aspirational to always consider ourselves a world port, even when steamboats could barely travel over a tree-choked bayou. It was aspirational to conceive of an air-conditioned baseball stadium. It was aspirational to start a small private college with the goal of being one of the premier institutions of higher learning in the country. Houstonians are so connected and networked, it seems like a small town. But because it is so open to all, the connections increase exponentially. In my experience, Dallas has spent several lifetimes looking over its shoulder at Houston, so it could congratulate itself for not being like Houston. Big deal. We're proud to be Houston.

SCOTT CLANTON

Scott Clanton, principal and owner of MG Architects in Houston, joined the firm in 1994. His professional experience includes commercial, retail, office, financial and religious facilities, as well as historic preservation. He has been the lead designer responsible for diverse projects including multi-story office, prototype branch banks, and LEED certified projects. The company was founded by architect Thompson McCleary in 1938, later becoming McCleary German Associates. and rebranding to MG in 2013 as part of their 75th anniversary.

From an architectural standpoint, Houston is very international. I don't think you can really put a label on Houston. Maybe "boom town" or "energy capital" but architecturally we're very diverse. We have designs from many cultures expressed here as well as modern and vernacular Texas styles. The lack of zoning is a double-edged sword here. It's good to be able to explore whatever you or your client want without too much interference. But some of the projects going up will take a toll. We have plenty of red tape with civic associations and architectural controls, but strict rules do not always produce positive results. There are several areas where civic associations or architectural controls are firmly in place. What you get in the end is bland and monotonous. We do a fair amount of work outside of Houston, so we get our fill of zoning elsewhere.

Some of the buildings that inspire me the most in Houston include:

- The Menil Collection: simple, clean, unassuming, fits into the neighborhood, almost upstages the art.
- Williams Tower (formerly Transco Tower) and water wall, great public space.
- The Bank of America Center (originally Republic Bank Tower).

Yes, it's Philip Johnson again, but the massing is interesting and the volume created on the inside is unexpected. Great natural lighting in those large open expanses.
- The James Turrell Skyspace at Rice University— it's almost not even there. For me, creating unexpected interior spaces and opportunities for natural lighting are important aspects of our design work.

While our clients want their projects to look nice, if it doesn't function or if it's not efficient, that's a problem. We're very pragmatic. We settle the functionality first and then focus on the form. They're not divorced concepts, however, and decisions are made in each category that certainly affect the other. It's like a chair—the chair can be the best looking chair you've ever seen, but if it's not comfortable, it's a fail.

Looking ahead 10 or 20 years, I'd like Houston to be a little cleaner and I wish we would take more pride as a city in keeping it clean—as simple as not throwing an entire bag from McDonald's out the car window. Though it's seemingly unpopular, I'd like to see light rail expanded—correctly. If we could plan routes to hit major nodes throughout the city I think it could be successful. I'd certainly be willing to use it to get to areas such as Downtown, NRG Stadium, airports or the Galleria.

Maybe we could do a better job of creating better buildings and environments by making decisions based on things other than just cost. I visited with a local developer last fall about some synergies we might have and he shared a few images of a two-building development he was preparing to create. During the process, I think his landscape architect suggested an alternative configuration that created a shared green space between the two buildings and pushed the parking elsewhere onto the site. This forced several other adjustments in the overall scheme and probably cost more. If he executes the plan, however, it will be a better development in the long run. And again, despite the outcome of the referendum, I'd like to see the Astrodome still on the map in 20 years.

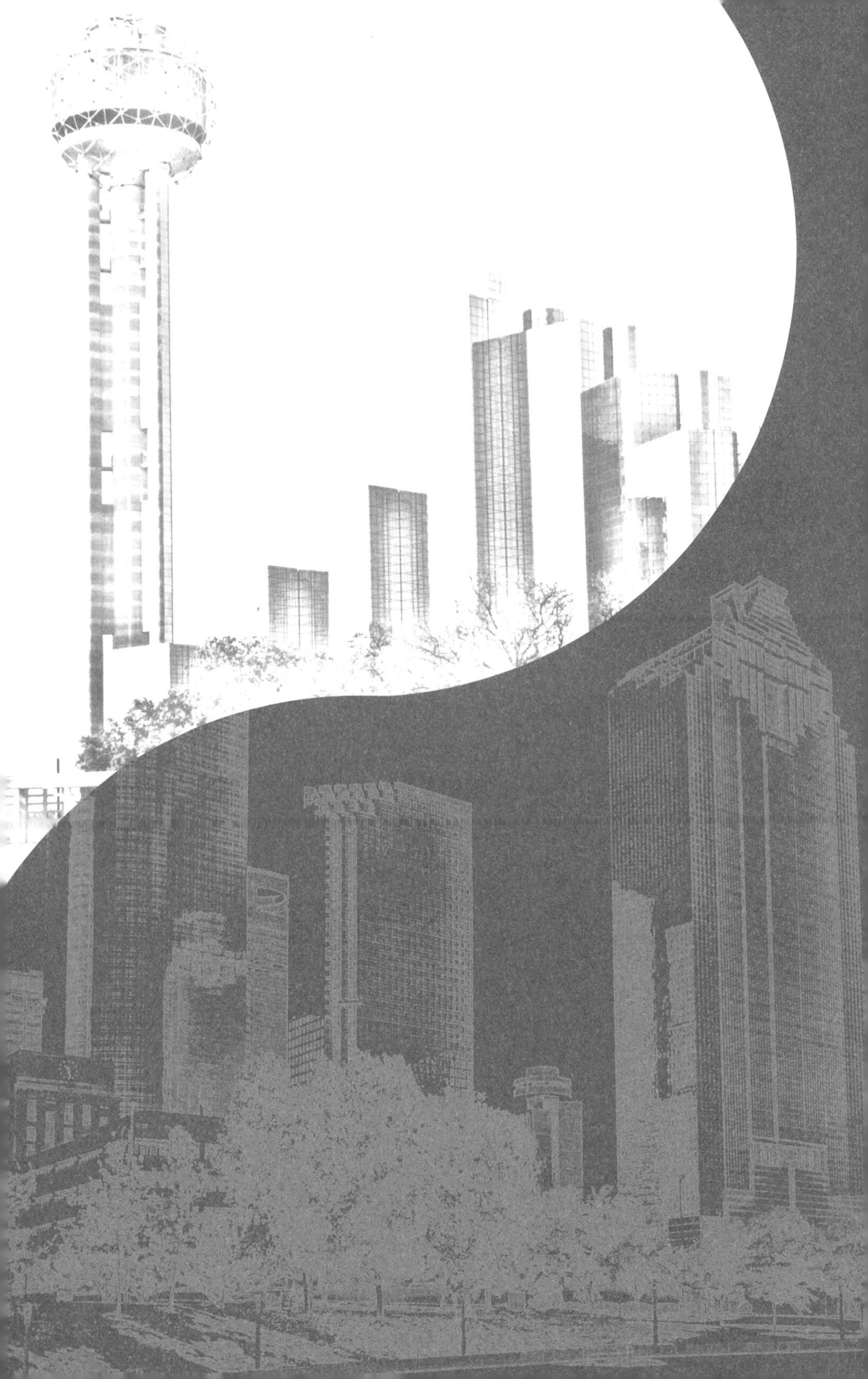

08

REAL ESTATE

Second only to iconic oil and gas, and hardly unrelated, dealing in real estate in Houston or Dallas is not for the faint of heart. It's a business in which it's possible to go from rags to riches more than once in a career. Few who lived through it can forget that period in the 1980s when downtown Houston resembled a really expensive, steel-and-glass ghost town. Still, with skill and luck and, as the success stories are quick to remind us, very long hours, many have found real estate the key to that Texas-sized version of the American Dream.

Let's face it: both in fiction and reality, Texans love real estate—the fact that you can buy it and sell it, the fact that you can touch the dirt whenever you want, the fact that you can boast that it's yours. Go back far enough and land was king, starting with those seemingly endlessly cattle ranches in West and South Texas that inspired Edna Ferber to write *Giant* and Elizabeth Taylor, Rock Hudson and James Dean to star in the movie. Eventually real estate holdings separated into commercial or residential, with developers, brokers and agents tending to specialize. Something about both types of real estate appealed to the Texas mind, the Texas desire to own and control.

More than most businesses, it seems, so many things about real estate are beyond anyone's control—the national, state and local economies first and foremost. Yet the fact remains that real estate is simply *real.* Texas men and women who spend 30, 40 or even 50 years buying and selling it successfully probably love that about it most of all.

MARTHA TURNER

A native of a tiny town in East Texas, Martha Turner has been the mater familias *of Houston real estate virtually since her company's beginnings in 1981. Her name has long been associated with the most elite transactions, though in recent years she has expanded her focus. She was invited by legendary Houston banker Ben Love to serve on his board of directors and, later, by Governor George W. Bush to join the Board of Regents of her alma mater, University of North Texas.*

Few people who've known me during my Houston real estate life would guess that I grew up in Hemphill, population 972, in East Texas not far from the Sabine River, or that the first thing I seriously tried to be was an opera singer. It was that dream that started me on the road to Houston, though I couldn't have guessed it at the time. It also started me on the road to real estate. That road has often been a roller coaster, as Houston enjoyed wild good times and, once in a while, wild bad times. I don't think I could have prospered, or

HOUSTON: *Highland Village*

even survived, without the grace of God and a bit of luck. Happily, Houston has been there to keep me supplied with both of those.

Looking at the world from Hemphill, the best place I could find to become an opera singer was the University of North Texas, which had a great music department. What I didn't know was that most of the people I'd be singing alongside had years of vocal training, music theory and a lot more skill on the piano than I'd been able to acquire. All of a sudden, I wasn't a big fish in a small pond but a small fish in a big pond. And that was *Denton*, not even Dallas. I had to step back and breathe.

Sometime around my senior year, I got the same advice that young women had been getting for generations: all this singing was fine but you'd better get a degree in elementary education. This I did, which allowed me to get a job teaching music in public schools when my husband was in law school in Austin. As to where we would live after that, I had many friends in Dallas but I'd felt pulled to Houston since I was a child. I'd been here for the ballet and the opera, and to see Gene Autry at what's now the Houston Livestock Show and Rodeo.

I taught school for 15 years, but all through that time my husband was a land developer. I built four new houses and remodeled two others—until one day I looked up at my family and said, "I want you to consider letting me resign as a teacher and go to real estate school." That was in 1978. So of course, I started getting into real estate in Houston just about the time it was getting ready to become the hardest job in the world. Many people I know lost everything in the 1980s, just as so many others would during the recession of 2008.

From the very beginning, lots of people told me I was crazy. They didn't know why I'd give up a good job like teaching, and they suggested I do real estate part-time. I told them that would be like going to a part-time surgeon or using a part-time attorney. Besides, as a youngster, I'd worked at the general store in Hemphill. I know nothing about any business except the words "May I help you, please."

In Houston we're famous for having no zoning. Sometimes that puts a real downer on houses on the front row in, close to all the commercial development, but it also has given us the ability to grow this city with no stops. Houston eases right out, annexes and grows. I don't think there's another city in this country that has a growth pattern like we have in Houston.

To me, the differences between Houston and Dallas are very clear. In Dallas you have to have many credentials—where you come from, who your parents were, where you went to school—to be accepted into certain circles. When you come to Houston, there's no real need for that. I think it's much more difficult for a Houstonian to move to Dallas than a Dallasite to move to Houston. The Dallasite coming here gets inundated with invitations to join all kinds of things. There are no barriers in Houston.

KAREN DERR

Karen Derr has been selling Houston area real estate since 1989, building a medium-sized real estate brokerage firm with 60 agents and three offices in Houston and Galveston. She has lived in Houston since she was in the second grade, much of that revolving around the historic inner-city neighborhood of Houston Heights. Developed north of downtown around 1900, it was Houston's first master planned community.

I think neighborhoods are particularly important to Houston because Houston is and has always been about business. The neighborhoods are cool shady oases to escape the ever-present crush of economic growth. If you think about it, the oil bust of the 1980s was less than a decade long here but it's been go-go-go the rest of the time. We really need places to rest and rejuvenate with family.

I think I have a feel for the temperament, flavor and even the politics of our neighborhood. My job is to help newcomers find the neighborhood that offers the comfort they are looking for. Believe me, Houston has something for everyone. The neighborhoods I naturally gravitate towards all have a sense of history, architecture or cultural interest. Neighborhood history is a framework people can find their place within. "My dad was against it but I like it…That was before my time but I'd like it without the gingerbread trim…My family was there…We came from a town like this." Even newcomers can find a neighborhood that provides a landmark pointing to where they are in their lives and where they are likely going.

My mother told me when I was little that Houston had no culture except the rodeo. Yet she loved it. It's come a long way since she came here in the 1950s in becoming a world-class cultural center. Let's face it, oil and gas are just a turnoff in general to some people; but they are fooling themselves if they don't think it fuels much of all of our lives in the whole Gulf Coast area. Houstonians face that fact head-on. That is our bohemian side: we take everything here with a dose of the grit of reality. Just because you don't work in oil and gas, doesn't mean you're not a part it if you live and work anywhere on the Gulf Coast.

In previous decades, I'd hear about California homes selling with ten offers on the first day and I'd say to myself, if that happened here my seller would say "Well, I guess we priced it too low." Now it's happening here and it a little daunting for everyone involved. Our greatest challenges are the same as other U.S. cities: corruption and stealing of resources that could be used to improve our infrastructure and the declining parts of our city. The areas where the monied live (and there are lots of these places) fund their own quality of life. The "best" places to live have private neighborhood policing, paid for by residents on top of their taxes. Every decade, we become more and more a city of "haves" and "have-nots," in my opinion. The future has some bright spots, though. We're officially the most diverse city in America. Besides racial diversity, our GLBT community is huge and well rooted. Houston was right there with New York and San Francisco in the struggle for equality way back in the 70s.

Houston heartily celebrates achievement and good ideas. Diversity breeds innovation, regardless of what the good ol' boys think. A lot of very successful realtors in Houston come from humble backgrounds, not bored wives of rich men, as is the stereotype. Real estate is a huge part of Houston's economy. Entrepreneurship here is so greatly rewarded, it's phenomenal. I feel where you came from just isn't as much of a hurdle here as it might be in other large cities.

NANCY ARREGUIN

With her business partner, Mexican entrepreneur and TV personality Carmina Zamorano, Nancy Arreguin runs a uniquely bilingual real estate business in Houston. Serving a clientele accustomed to pampering, she has created an amalgam of agent and concierge that seems to make many people happy.

I had the pleasure of meeting Carmina while working on a real estate transaction that I completed a few years ago. We instantly clicked and were able to form a bond that blossomed into this partnership. Through this business, we are able to positively impact the lives of many Houstonians today and contribute to this city's successful real estate market. Right now Houston is so hot. Every listing out there has three to five offers. I have relationships with different realtors in New York City and California, and even though they are doing very well, they are shocked by the number of offers we get here. It means you have to be quick. I'm sending listings out to my buyers at one or three in the morning. And that's because I get alerts—thank God for technology.

To my way of thinking, Carnan Properties is a company that suits all nationalities and cultures in and out of Houston, but our company has seen particular success from interaction with foreign nationals. The United States, and especially Houston, is a melting pot of foreigners that come here to seek change, success and opportunities. I have been blessed to also benefit from their opportunities as I help them settle into life in a new city and sometimes even a new country. Every single client I've had, I'm friends with now.

As a bilingual company, we are especially good at working with people who speak Spanish and Portuguese, with Mexicans making up the single largest group; but we work with other nationalities as well. There are ten or more flights into Houston each day from different cities in Mexico, so it is very convenient for those who have businesses in Mexico and want to commute from Houston every week. Still, even in our short time doing this, we've also helped Nigerians, French and Vietnamese.

When they arrive in Houston, the one thing all of our clients have in common is a heightened expectation of service. And that is something not every real estate office is willing or able to give them. These are people who are used to having people do for them, so in our concierge mode we work very hard to give them the level of service they expect. We help make reservations in restaurants, get them tickets to Texans games, find them nannies or bodyguards—anything that can facilitate what they're trying to do in their lives. We've even had a few people buy a house for their wife and an apartment for their girlfriend!

Since I started in this business when I was in college, working with my father as he was flipping houses, I've had enough to time to see a few changes in the Houston market—or at least in the market we strive to serve. Recently, we have had two of the most expensive listings in Tanglewood, one for $6 million and one for $4.5 million. The type of people who can buy such a residence expect customer service 24 hours a day. Trust me, they're not used to realtors not answering their phones or answering emails because it's 7 p.m. in the evening.

HENRY S. MILLER IV

Henry S. Miller III grew up in the Dallas real estate business founded by his grandfather and greatly expanded by his father; his son Henry Miller IV now plays a significant role in the company. The family counts Highland Park Village and the newer mixed-use West Village among its proudest accomplishments, along with founding the Dallas Opera and helping guide the Dallas Symphony and Dallas Ballet through difficult times.

I can think of many things that make Dallas unique. For one thing, we have for the most part enjoyed a long-term period of uninterrupted growth in development, population, business openings and new housing between downtown and just about as far north as you'd want to go. There's a kind of corridor there that has not, even with the economic downturn, stopped growing and improving as far back as I can remember, and I've been in the business since 1968.

We've also been fortunate enough to have really enterprising developers who have been interested not only in their own business but

---

DALLAS: *Highland Park Village*

in improving the city. The quality and innovation of these developers is, I think, second to none. For instance, Northpark Mall was built by Ray Nasher back in the early 60s, and there are many ways he could have developed it and turned a profit faster. Today Northpark is very much in the middle of things, but it was all agricultural property back then. Ray Nasher developed it in such a way that it enhanced the whole area. Instead of simply bringing in Sears or a Penney's as an anchor store, according to one of several formulas, and just letting the rest of the leasing happen around that, he spent a fortune on architecture, planning and impact analysis. Northpark created an entire focus on upscale fashion that set it apart, and it was one of the first examples in the country of a high-end regional shopping mall.

Although it's smaller than Northpark, I'm also proud of a project we developed, West Village on McKinney Avenue. It's open-air, and it was actually one of the first major mixed-use projects done in Texas. It created a pedestrian space with residential, retail, restaurants and entertainment that brought in the whole neighborhood. When we started it in 1997, we were told by a lot of people that it would never work, that people here would insist on driving and parking in front of each store. Indeed, I remember watching people come out of one store—say Chanel—get in their cars and drive a short distance down the row, park and go into another store. We tried, successfully I believe, to change the habits of people and give them an experience that was richer.

Especially during the five years I spent in Houston in the 1970s, everybody was always asking me about zoning—since Dallas has a fairly traditional zoning system and Houston is proud to tell you it has none. I was always asked the impact of this on growth. In Houston, when I was there, I think there was more opportunity to create unusual, interesting developments simply because it was allowed. I'm not sure that the way the Galleria has happened in Houston, with its mixture of uses, would have taken place in a traditional zoning format. Now Dallas has gotten past much of that and has been able to do some interesting things. Plus, planned developments have allowed a little more flexibility.

These days Dallas is a city that has attracted people from all over the country and all over the world. Instead of just building more and more of the same homogenous neighborhoods, people are focusing more on diversity and the mixing of our many cultures. I see people planning things now, and they're looking at the impact on cultures, at the impact on the entire community, much more than they ever would have in the past. That gives me a great deal of hope for the future.

ROBBIE BRIGGS

The second generation to give the family name to one of the city's leading brokerage firms for residential real estate, Robbie Briggs is now president and CEO of Briggs Freeman Sotheby's International Realty. Since 1980, he has translated a master's degree in architecture from Tulane University into the natural venue of real estate. The company has six offices in the Metroplex and 220 associates.

While we enjoy a tremendous quality of life here in Dallas, we realize that dramatic growth is more than pretty parks, a striking skyline and a place to enjoy sporting events. As a region, the Metroplex's strength is in its numbers. Growth in every sector—business, culture, medicine—means a better quality of life in neighborhoods, schools and communities.

In terms of the arts, culture and impact, Dallas' Arts District is the largest contiguous arts district in the country, drawing more than 1.5 million ticketed visitors a year and creating more than $128 million worth of economic impact. Investments of more than $300 million in downtown, including the Klyde Warren Park and the Perot Museum of Nature and Science, reportedly will bring more than $1.2 billion in income from business and real estate growth. In nearby For Worth, the Kimbell Art Museum is undergoing a $125 million expansion that will add to the economic impact of arts in the city, which currently stands at $241 million annually.

In the field of medicine, UT Southwestern Medical Center currently contributes a combined impact of approximately $1.6 billion to the region and more than 23,000 jobs. The campus' new University Hospital, an $800 million, state of the art facility, is slated to open in 2015. Baylor Health Care System opened Baylor Medical Center at

McKinney in July 2012, spending just over $200 million and creating over 500 jobs. Cook Children's Hospital completed a $250 million expansion impacting children across Tarrant County.

There are plenty of exciting things on the horizon for the Dallas-Fort Worth area. The proposed Trinity Forest Golf Club is projected to bring more than $32 million annually in economic impact to southern Dallas. With a $2 billion investment by Beck Ventures and the new name "Dallas Midtown," the Valley View area will undergo a major renovation over the next ten years. Over $5.2 billion has poured into Dallas-area development so far in 2013, a 21% increase over the same period in 2012. The largest projects include the $113 million T5 office space addition at the Dallas Data Center in Plano, a new $91 million high school campus in the suburb of Flower Mound and several warehouse sites that will serve as distribution centers for companies like Nebraska Furniture Mart, ACE Hardware and Amazon. Toyota announced in 2014 it was moving its U.S. Headquarters from Southern California to Plano, along with 4,000 people. It is estimated that the economic impact for this will be $7.2 billion for the region over ten years.

I think Dallas is a great city in which to do business and raise a family. The city is friendly, welcoming and entrepreneurial, and it has made great strides in becoming world class. The people of Dallas are resilient, creative, educated and connected. Dallas is an incubator for innovation, from Texas Instruments to potato chips. Dallas is highly diversified. Houston is also a great city, which adds to the strength of our state. All of our cities have very different strengths and personalities, and that is what makes Texas great.

ALLIE BETH ALLMAN

Since 1985, the name Allie Beth Allman has been synonymous with the best estates, high-profile clientele, and superior customer service in the Dallas luxury real estate market. 2012 was a record year, as Allie Beth Allman & Associates became the first single office firm in Dallas history to sell $1 billion worth of real estate in Highland Park, University Park, Preston Hollow and surrounding Dallas neighborhoods.

08: REAL ESTATE

The hardest thing about being in real estate, in Dallas or probably anywhere else, is that everybody thinks they can do it—and without working at it much. I think I have a talent for selling—always have, even when I was a little girl. But I also know I've perfected it by working every day. Real estate is a lot of work, and it's hard. It's a major investment for people to do it right, and it seems like a lot of them don't realize it when they get in.

Texas doesn't have any income tax and it does have oil income, which explains why people keep moving here, to Dallas and every other part of the state. And as long as people keep moving here, that of course is good for the real estate business. Nobody moves to Dallas for the climate or the view. People love the ocean and the mountains, but we don't have that here. What we have is great people and great business opportunities.

I think Dallas has something for everyone. It's the 3rd largest city in Texas and the 9th largest in the United States. It's also the largest economic center of the 12-county Dallas-Fort Worth Metroplex that is the largest metropolitan area in the South and 4th-largest in the United States. Founded in 1841 and formally incorporated in 1856, the city's economy is primarily based on banking, commerce, telecommunications, computer technology, energy and transportation. Dallas is home to several Fortune 500 companies. The city's prominence arose from its historical importance as a center for the oil and cotton industries and its position along numerous railroad lines. Dallas developed a strong industrial and financial sector, and a major inland port, due largely to the presence of Dallas-Fort Worth International Airport, one of the largest and busiest in the world. It was rated as a beta world city by the Globalization and World Cities Study Group & Network.

There are always ups and downs in real estate, so I don't look to the future or the past—just to what we're working on today. If we all had a magic wand and a crystal ball, we'd all be rich.

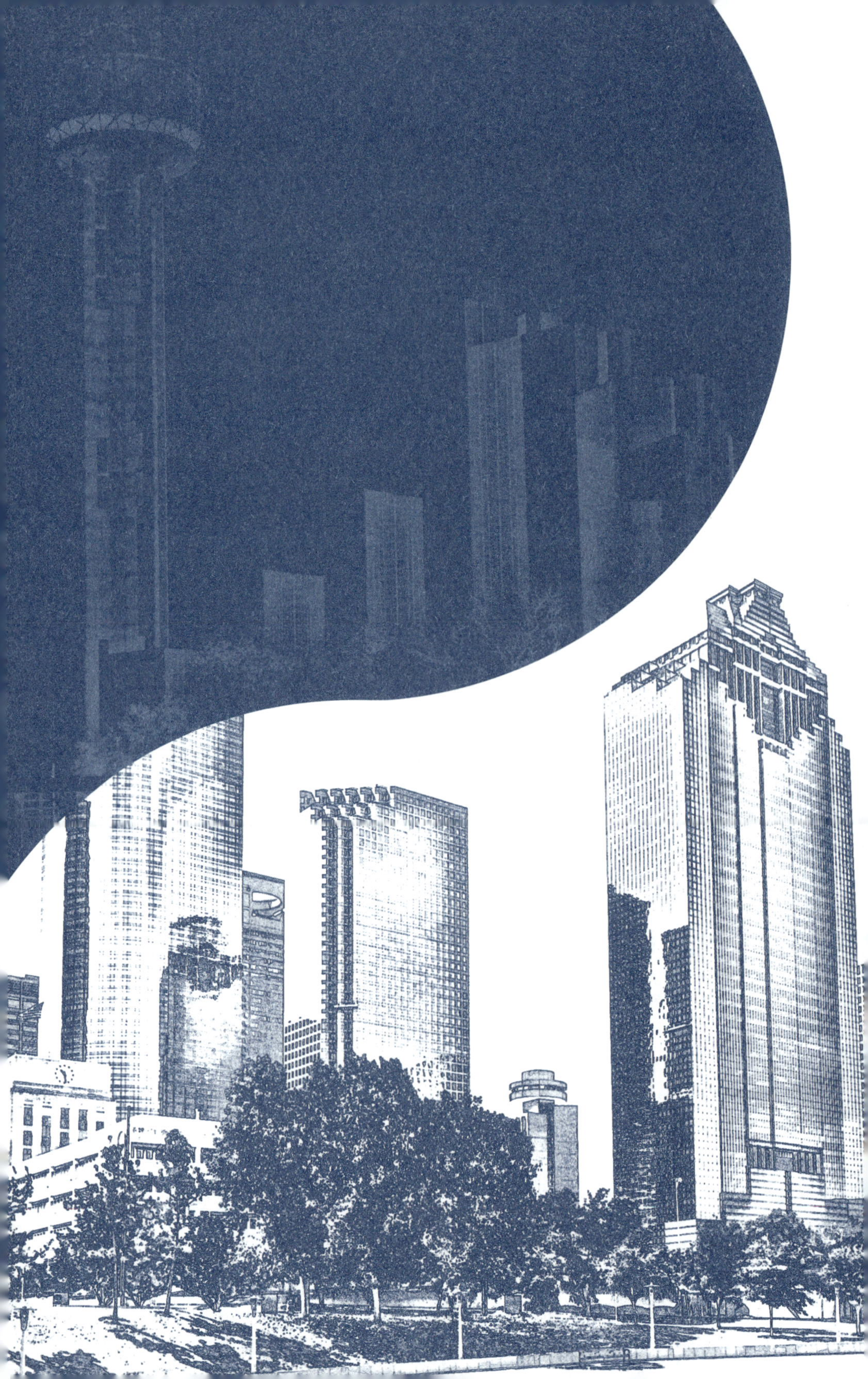

RESTAURANTS

There are still many visitors who arrive in Texas and wonder where the nearest chili or barbecue might be. And thanks to hundreds of traditional Texas restaurants, they seldom have to look very hard to find some. But in the past two to three decades, the cooking revolution that has transformed America has transformed Texas, too. To say that huge sections of this revolution have been "chef-driven" is an understatement.

In Houston and Dallas, we are now on at least our second generation of chefs—real generation, not just stylistic wave—who take their training seriously and their passionate self-expression even more so. Often with expertise developed at places like the Culinary Institute of America or Johnson and Wales, these chefs feel empowered to reinterpret and perhaps even reinvent the cooking Texans grew up eating by way of techniques and ingredients borrowed from France first and foremost, but also Italy, Spain and Asia. The result in both cities is a dining scene that changes as fast as the Texas weather, with fan clubs following their favorite chefs, like rock stars, from one location to another.

The explosion of multi-ethnic populations in Houston and Dallas also contributes to and enriches the dining scene, giving diners the basics on each traditional cuisine so they understand what the upscale chefs are doing. There is still plenty of chicken fried steak served in Houston and Dallas, thank goodness. But you can't be too sure what might turn up on the plate beside it.

TONY VALLONE

Since 1965, through boom, bust and no small number of food fads, Tony Vallone has operated Houston's most revered fine-dining restaurant. A saucier trained in the French tradition, Vallone has devoted his life to serving elite guests the highest levels of Italian cuisine. With his wife Donna, he has breathed life into several other restaurant concepts over the decades—Anthony's, Vallone's, La Griglia, Grotto—but his ever-pampering Tony's remains home.

In a way, I learned all I needed to know about Houston as a place for business in the first years after opening the original Tony's in 1965, almost half a century ago. It was a very small Italian restaurant, totally Mom and Pop, in a city where it was hard to get so many of the foods we all take for granted now. There were no fresh clams or mussels, so I had to make many of the classic Italian dishes using oysters. I had to go to a bait camp to get calamari. But I had good food and worked my butt off round the clock. And Gerald Hines, my landlord for 40 years until we moved here, liked what he saw. We leased

HOUSTON: *Cordúa*

month-to-month from him for the first seven years. Then when he told us we had to move so he could build the Galleria, he found us a space on Post Oak and helped us get financing. I remember him telling me: I want this to be the best restaurant in Houston. This city is all about people like Gerald Hines.

Houston is a city of arts and opportunity, with the world's largest and best medical center, the nation's second-largest port, first place in the nation in exportation and creation of jobs, magnificent theater, arts and museum districts, frequent and diverse street festivals and great restaurants. Anything one can want or enjoy can be found in this great city. It's a can-do city open to all, welcoming and unpretentious yet vibrant and diverse. These are just a few of the things that make Houston one of the great cities in this hemisphere.

In my own case, pioneering fine dining here was made much easier by being in this accepting, welcoming and savoring cosmopolitan city. Houston is open-minded when it comes to things that are new and creative and always ready to reward talent and hard work. Houstonians are always ready to help the innovative entrepreneur. It's easy to be inspired and driven here, knowing that in Houston perseverance and attention to detail really do pay off.

It's very difficult for me to define only a few moments in Houston—this great tapestry of talent, hard work and creativity. Attracting and keeping Fortune 500 companies, petrochemical giants, a comprehensive and nurturing medical center, a bustling port and museums to rival anywhere in America all come together to create memorable moments in our civic and charitable history. Houstonians' lifestyles can be crafted to any desired way of life: slow and relaxing or fast and vibrant. There is something for everyone here.

Things that set Houston apart from all other cities include beautiful areas, diverse architecture, lush greenery, well-placed parks, a friendly, open atmosphere and a willingness for constant refinement. World-class shopping certainly adds to the city's allure. Houston is an assured and confident city that has no need to boast or brag, unlike its little sister to the north. Houstonians have always had good palates. Everything is here. You cannot run a restaurant from a boardroom in Cleveland or from a golf course or from a gala. When you go to a restaurant and you see an owner working, you know it's a good restaurant.

ROBERT DEL GRANDE

With his Ph.D. in biochemistry in hand, Robert del Grande left his native California in 1981 to chase his future bride Mimi to Houston. He ended up cooking at a restaurant she owned with her sister and brother-in-law, Café Annie. In recent years, that beloved Houston culinary destination has evolved into RDG + Bar Annie. Del Grande and chef Dean Fearing (of Dallas) play music in a band called the Barbwires.

I always sort of *got* the whole Houston-Dallas thing because I was born in California, in San Francisco. And people were always talking about us and Los Angeles—why this or that city was better, why this or that one was the "real California." The only thing was: L.A. had Disneyland, and there was really nothing we could say to that. Just like Dallas had J.R. and that TV show. But I'm glad I had this idea about Dallas because I ended up working with two chef friends there, Dean Fearing and Stephan Pyles, to promote the stuff we were doing. It ended up being called Southwestern Cuisine, but among us, it was *Texas* Cuisine. The three of us were always in New York or Chicago or L.A., talking about the food we were doing back home in Texas.

I remember when I first arrived in Houston, I'd actually been in L.A. for a while, so I knew both the cities out there well, and there was a lot of excitement about food—about so-called California Cuisine. Even there it was all new, kind of inspired by French *nouvelle cuisine*, by the Troisgros brothers, Michel Guerard and those guys. I found the very same stuff was exciting chefs here in Houston. For a long time, I understood, there was French but mostly Continental cuisine in very fancy settings, often in the big hotels. All the service in such places was tableside, with waiters carving this and flaming that. We young chefs set out to change that.

The first thing I remember loving here was barbecue, which was real Texas barbecue, not California barbecue, which is hamburgers in the backyard. I loved the rustic quality, the sense of place. Most of all, I loved the music coming over the speakers. There was a tie between the food and the sound that captured me. I was also reading everything that came out on food. Not surprisingly, I was always the guy with a book under his arm.

As the whole Southwestern thing took off, I remember asking Dean one time if he ever wondered what would happen if it didn't work. He said, "Nope." I was trying to do local things—not just the local produce idea but the local *idea*. I was more interested in what would make people say, "That's the way they do it in Houston." Many chefs, in the 80s, were copying things being done in New York. The three of us were trying to do something that New York was going to copy. And with Southwestern Cuisine, it pretty much worked out that way.

Overall today, Houston is a fairly young and vibrant dining city. Many people are doing good stuff. Since it's a laidback city, you don't have to have pomp and circumstance to be really good. And all the ethnic restaurants contribute by opening people's minds to a wide variety of new ingredients. When I started, nobody here even knew what radicchio was. Now I'm not sure you can surprise anybody with anything.

We're still trying to cook local food, and by that we mean *food* that's local, not just ingredients. I think about local sourcing, since we do a lot of it. But it still doesn't make sense to tell a customer you won't serve him raspberries in the dead of winter because they're "out of season." That would be ideological, saying he *can't* or *shouldn't* eat them because the only raspberries you have come from, say, Chile. He'll look at you like you're an idiot and say, "Of course they're in season. I just saw them at the grocery." Sometimes I think: Hey, I could fly from Houston to Chile and be allowed to eat a raspberry there because it's in season. Or I could just eat one here. It's easier and cheaper to fly that raspberry to me than it is to fly me to that raspberry.

MICHAEL CORDÚA

Along with his son, Chef David Cordúa, Michael Cordúa is the culinary force behind a collection of restaurants in the Houston area specializing in Latin flavors. Beginning with Churrascos a quarter-century ago, the Cordúas now also have locations of Américas, Artista and Amazón Grill. And yes, they do plan on expanding to Dallas.

You might say I got to meet Houston for the first time twice: first when I arrived from Nicaragua via Texas A&M to start my shipping career, and again more than 25 years ago to slip into a chef jacket and launch my first restaurant. Especially from the perspective of cooking and serving people at Churrascos, Américas, Artista and Amazón Grill, I have seen so many changes. Yet Houston is still very much Houston, a diverse and dynamic city that cares more about what you can do than who your parents are or where you came from. I'm convinced that's the key to Houston's success. Since it's quite different from my world growing up in Nicaragua, I had every reason to notice.

We in Houston are not given the credit for everything we do well and right. The fact that we're branded as cowboys, especially by people outside Texas, doesn't do justice to all the cultures we have here. This is a world-class city, whose greatest aspiration these days is to demonstrate the richness of our cultures.

Houston was not at all as diverse when I first came here, and certainly not in the types of restaurants that were available—a fact that played a big part in our beginnings in the business. In population, there were the Tex-Mex, African-American and Anglo communities—that was about it. And to eat, there was not much more than barbecue, steak, very Americanized Italian and Tex-Mex. Yet Houston has always been open and embracing, because it has always needed people to come and work. We are a city in which someone can come and work two or three jobs just to make ends meet, and then his or her children or grandchildren can be the first in their family to go to college.

Yes, we are looking to open a restaurant in Dallas, perhaps before we open in other Texas cities. But that's always been a tough border to cross. There are almost no Dallas restaurants doing well in Houston and almost no Houston restaurants doing well in Dallas. For instance, two great friends—Robert del Grande and Dean Fearing—have never opened fine dining restaurants in each other's cities, and Stephan Pyles hasn't opened a place in Houston either. Yet when we Houstonians travel to Dallas, we always go to those restaurants.

During my years traveling from Houston to other American cities and other countries in the shipping business, I learned how to be more adventurous in what I ate, in places like New York or London, and across different parts of Latin America. In those days, such an education would not have happened in Houston—I mean, *sushi?*—but now it happens here to everybody who wants it, every day. I'd like to think our restaurants have played a small role in that evolution, demonstrating there was so much more to Latin food than Tex-Mex. It was five years before we dared serve anything that involved a tortilla, just to avoid the confusion—even when we were always eating tortillas in the kitchen.

DEAN FEARING

Dean Fearing opened the Mansion on Turtle Creek for Carolyn Hunt in 1980 and, with only a three-year stint at Agnew's, cooked food famously there until 2006. One of the fathers of Southwestern Cuisine, Fearing now operates Fearing's at the Ritz-Carlton Hotel.

When I came to Dallas in 1979, it was to work as a *poissonier* at the Fairmont Hotel's Pyramid Room—a French "fish cook" in a French restaurant in a town that respected French food. As a sign of those times, I was coming to Dallas from another French restaurant in Cincinnati. It was assumed back then that if you mattered in Dallas, you went to Paris and the rest of France at least once or twice a year, to eat in all the Michelin three-star restaurants. And when you weren't going to France, you were going to New York, where you generally were eating French food as well. The New York restaurants that Dallas people talked about all had names like La Côte Basque and La Grenouille, plus a place called the 21 Club that would play a

DALLAS: *Fearing's Restaurant at the Ritz-Carlton*

part in my Dallas life. So at the Pyramid Room, I cooked nothing but French under a chef who was French.

It was that chef, in fact, who showed me an article about Carolyn Hunt taking an old mansion and turning it into a restaurant. Since I wanted to be a saucier and he was a saucier with no plans to leave, he suggested I might have better luck down the street. We opened in July 1980, with management by that same 21 Club out of New York. It was the perfect setting for Dallas to sink its teeth in.

I might still be cooking French in Dallas if only the French chef at the Mansion had been willing to work nights. Instead, he came in early and left around 5:30 p.m., handing me the keys and letting me run the dinner show, which was the greatest thing in the whole wide world. As night sous chef, I had to create all the specials, and that meant the type of dishes my idol at the time, Wolfgang Puck, was doing out in Los Angeles at Ma Maison. He was using French techniques but also lots of American techniques. One day Mrs. Hunt came into the kitchen and handed the chef a piece of scratch paper with two words written on it: "tortilla soup." The chef hated the whole idea but we put tortilla soup on the menu.

Over the years that followed, I left the Mansion when some wealthy investors lured me off to create Agnew's in the "middle of nowhere" in north Dallas. It was there that Craig Claiborne of *The New York Times* came to dinner, and then only because one of our owners took a car to get him. He said he'd have only one course—I remember it was roasted yellow bell pepper soup with serrano cream—but he ended up staying through dessert, and later came back to Dallas to feature our the recipes on the front page of his food section.

I ended up back at the Mansion after the investors went broke and Agnew's closed, and I stayed until leaving to create Fearing's at the Ritz-Carlton in 2006. For a good while there, the Southwestern Cuisine that was born to some degree with that first fine-dining tortilla soup had Stephan Pyles, Robert del Grande and me crisscrossing the country as celebrity chefs. I don't cook that food anymore—I call what I do "no rules, no borders" because our menu has Japanese dishes and even a curry. But for a while, people came to Dallas from all over everywhere for dinner, just like New York. And just like Paris.

KENT RATHBUN

Chef Kent Rathbun is the culinary force behind the fine-dining restaurant concept Abacus in Dallas and Jasper's Gourmet Backyard Cuisine in Plano, The Woodlands and Austin, along with a catering venue in Frisco, a catering and food company. He is also a partner with his wife, Tracy, and Lynae Fearing in Shinsei, a hip pan-Asian restaurant.

I came to Dallas to work at the Mansion on Turtle Creek with Dean Fearing. It was 1990 and I'd never cooked anywhere quite like it—certainly not my hometown of Kansas City, which was smaller and less affluent, and certainly not New Orleans. Then as now, New Orleans went its own way when it came to food. People I knew made sure I understood what a great opportunity this was, but it was still a leap of faith. I wanted it enough that I took a substantial cut in pay and dropped from executive chef to sous chef so I could make my way to Dallas.

Chefs here were doing some of the most awesome food I've ever seen in my life—Dean Fearing, of course, and Stephan Pyles, and Richard Chamberlain. There was a whole lot going on that interested me. You might say Abacus was born because I was in Dallas, even though I knew before I came that I wanted to open my own restaurant. That was my goal and probably would have happened anywhere, but when Abacus opened in 1999, Dallas offered a level of success that would have happened only in certain American cities. It helped me understand, from the caliber of business done in this city, that I was really interested in competing not only in Dallas but also on a national level. I felt like I could run in that circle.

The name Abacus was part of our game plan from the beginning—instead of something like McKinney Avenue. We wanted something that would be understood far outside of Dallas, all across the country. We had an idea the restaurant would be successful, but when you're putting in that kind of money and time and effort there's always a concern about it working at the level needed.

Dallas always supports its chefs. That's one thing we were counting on: the clientele in Dallas is very protective of its own. If you look at some of the failures of these big restaurant companies from

New York or Las Vegas, some of it may be their attitude. But I think it's because the people here really love their chefs—more than any other place I've ever worked. And they put their money where their mouth is.

I'm very optimistic about the future of Dallas–or maybe it's more like ecstatic. I've had the opportunity to work with the convention and visitors bureau here, seeing plans for some really awesome projects over the next two to ten years. I'm excited as a business owner, and I'm excited as a citizen. As this city continues to grow, our plan is to grow with it. The train's already headed down the track. The only question is: Did we get on at the right time?

DOTTY GRIFFITH

A native of Terrell, Texas, Dotty Griffith covered the food and restaurant scene for The Dallas Morning News *from 1972 to 2006, being "on the story" during the years that Southwestern Cuisine became a national fascination. The author of several food books, including* Celebrating Barbecue *and* The Texas Holiday Cookbook, *she now serves as executive director of the Greater Dallas Restaurant Association.*

When I started at the *Morning News* as food editor, it was really the time that the restaurant scene in Dallas and other similar cities was just starting to blossom, to be conscious of all the possibilities. This was, of course, driven by changes in Texas law that allowed liquor-by-the-drink and especially wine. When people were toting bourbon into restaurants in a plastic bag and ordering Coca-Cola as a set-up, it wasn't particularly conducive to fine dining. When there was fine wine in restaurants that could be paired with lovely food, it became a whole new scene.

There was a receptiveness among the public to all that was new and exciting in food. They loved anything having to do with the Gang of Five—which included three chefs who are still going strong, Dean Fearing and Stephan Pyles in Dallas and Robert del Grande in Houston—who were focusing on creating regional flavors. At the beginning, there was still a good deal of focus on exotic ingredients from somewhere else, but always with some kind of local spin. This was the time of mesquite-smoked everything. And chiles were in every dish anybody served back then—fresh, smoked, dried or whatever else.

There was something of a rift in the chef community between the older, more traditional, mostly European chefs still doing Continental cuisine and these new guys, who were getting all the media attention and who felt like they were moving dining forward. The consumers embraced the new completely, knowing that *we* had to love what people were coming from all over the country to taste. After all, Craig Claiborne of *The New York Times* liked it. Dallas has always been and probably always will be a place that loves seeing and being seen in a hot restaurant.

When I started covering food, Dallas was still very parochial, and it only over time became a world-class city with so much terrific art, music and architecture. In the 80s, it had some nouveau riche growing pains, all big hair and shoulder pads and in the spotlight from *Dallas* the TV show. But the city was also growing up. We are in a new era now, with not nearly so much ostentation. Dallas is a little more sure of itself, and it's definitely settling into its own skin.

I don't think Dallas gets the respect it deserves as a food city, and perhaps that's because it can be hard to tell our narrative in a way people can understand. Sometimes, unlike Austin or San Antonio or Houston, it's easier to say what Dallas isn't than what Dallas is. That's certainly one of my goals with the restaurant association, to use food and our chefs, new on the scene or here forever, to tell our city's story.

Right now, there's a younger generation of chefs doing all kinds of new and interesting things, shaking things up just like Dean and Stephan did back then. They're not united by the goal of Southwestern Cuisine, but they certainly have shared interests. They have a 21st-century mindset. They're doing less formal restaurants and less formal food. The chef community in Dallas has a whole new energy about it. We all want Dallas to be a culinary destination again, as it was during that first great culinary Camelot.

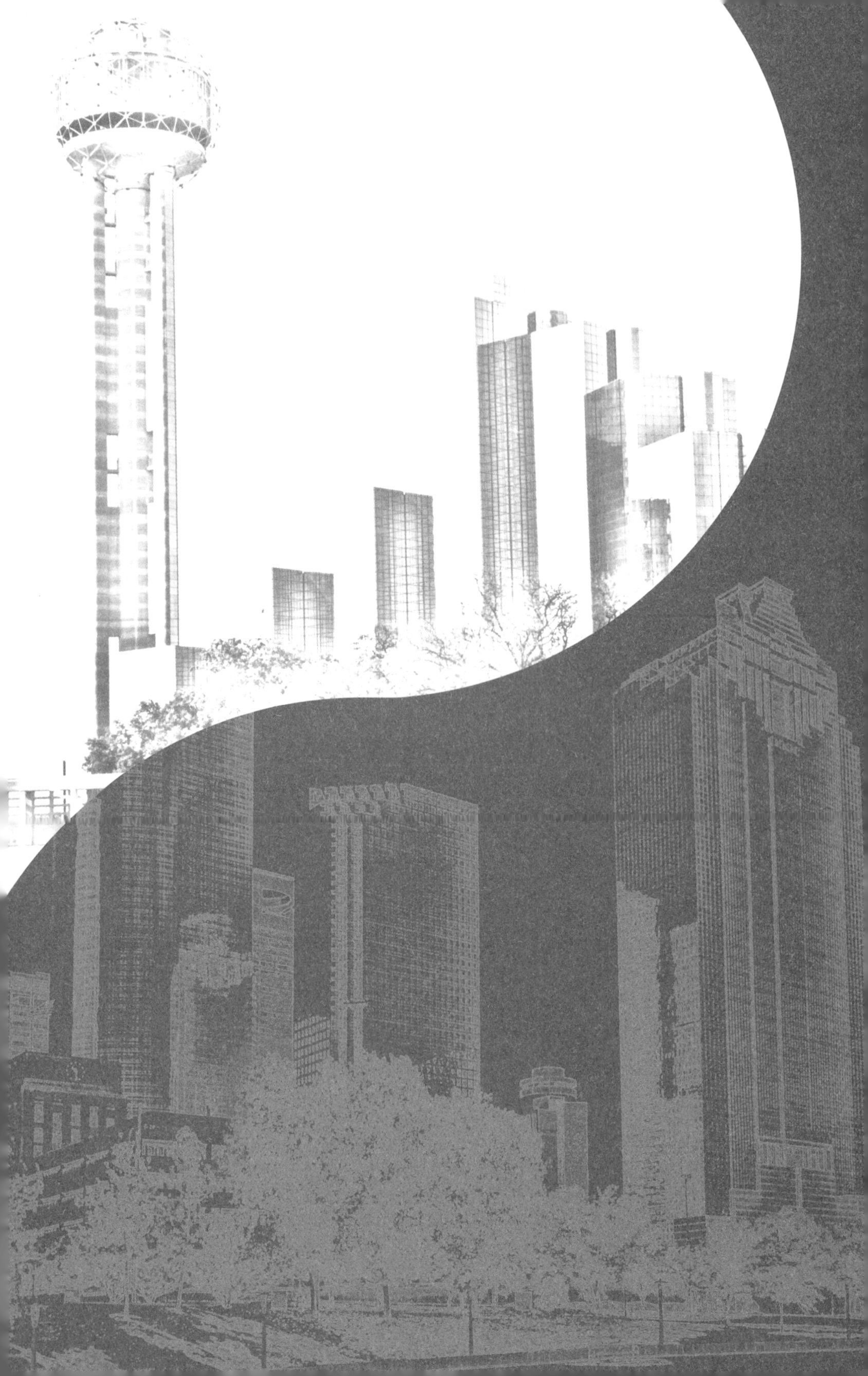

SPORTS

Dallas and Houston—they're a tale of two cities trying to one-up each other, and where could that happen better than in the naturally competitive arena of sports. In a sense, through good seasons and bad, Dallas wears its heart more on its sleeve with the Cowboys than Houston does with any of its teams. Houston fans, to most observers, are more about results, multiplying or dividing in number based on the W-L record. Cowboy fans follow the team like they're a religion.

Still, though NFL football has largely displaced Major League Baseball as the national pastime and the Houston Texans keep promising to get better, both cities are proud to possess all the team sports a major city might want. So, yes, football season is all about the Cowboys or the Texans, depending on your color scheme, but basketball is about the Mavericks or the Rockets, and baseball is about the Rangers or the Astros. When you get right down to it, and factor in college sports as well, there aren't too many days in a year that will leave the sports fan in Dallas or Houston with nobody to cheer for or grumble about.

JAIME ARON

Jaime Aron is a sports writer who was born and bred in Houston, but whose professional expertise covers all things Dallas. His most popular books include: Breakthrough 'Boys: When the Dallas Cowboys Went from Next Year's Champions to America's Team, The Complete Illustrated History of the Dallas Cowboys, *and* Best Dallas-Fort Worth Sports Arguments.

It's amazing to think of all the people who've brought some shine to the Dallas Cowboys' star, and those who've shined because of it. There are superstar players (Lilly, Roger, Troy, Emmitt) and colorful players (Dandy Don, Walt Garrison, Hollywood), legendary coaches (Tom, Jimmy, Parcells) and other characters (Jerry, Tex, every cheerleader, even Crazy Ray). Yet you know who I consider the club's most defining character? The guy who also may be the most important, and the most overlooked. The founder: Clint Murchison Jr.

I say this purely in retrospect. I never met the guy, never even discussed him with those who knew him. This notion is completely

DALLAS: *AT&T Stadium*

unbiased and completely viewed through the prism of history. As a Cowboys fan growing up in Houston (yes, that's true—while my generation was Lovin' Ya Blue, I cherished my Billy Joe DuPree T-shirt and agonized when Jackie Smith dropped that pass), I knew of Murchison. Ditto for my formative days as a sports writer. It wasn't until working on my first book, *I Remember Tom Landry*, that I began to gain a fondness for Clint Murchison.

Let's start with a few facts: Clint is the guy who knew pro football and Dallas were meant to be. He shrewdly got the NFL to give him an expansion team in 1960 and launched a delicious, devilish rivalry with the Redskins. (Keywords for your Google search on this subject: song rights, bribe, chickens.) When he got tired of his team's old, rickety stadium, he got a suburb to build him a palace unlike anything anyone had ever seen.

A few Clint stories: Before a game against the Giants, long before sellouts were common, Clint sent tickets to famed New York restaurateur Toots Shor—10,000 of 'em. Before the Cowboys' first game in Chicago, Clint hired a guy dressed up like a cowboy to "shoot" a bear that would then fall down. Following the PR stunt, Clint brought the pretend cowboy and the real bear up to his party room...and got them both drunk. Clint gave Tom a 10-year contract to quiet critics. He later said, "I do not offer suggestions to Landry. Furthermore, Landry never makes suggestions as to how I conduct my sixth-grade football team—which, incidentally, is undefeated. We have a professional standoff."

A big part of his legacy is evident in that last nugget; he stayed out of the way. He hired Tex Schramm to run the organization, and Tex in turn hired Tom to run the locker room. That strict chain of command led to 20 straight winning seasons. I don't need to tell you what the new chain of command has produced since the late 1990s.

Funny thing is, Clint and Jerry share many similarities: Smart and shrewd. Oil tycoons who tried at a young age to own the NFL team in Dallas, only to actually do it years later. All-Pro carousers. I asked Jerry once about putting Clint in the Ring of Honor. He said it had been considered. I followed up by asking about their similarities. He smiled and said he'd heard that before. Before I could get to that one major difference (hands-on vs. hands-off), Jerry made it clear we were done discussing it. What a shame. Ol' Clint started something that turned out to be pretty memorable, and it seems to me that he deserves to be better remembered too.

NORM HITZGES

Norm Hitzges hosted the first full-time sports talk-show in morning drive time in the country. He has been on-air continuously for nearly four decades in the DFW market. Known for his enthusiasm and knowledge of sports trivia, he has been honored by the Radio Hall of Fame, the Dallas Hall of Sports Association and the Texas Baseball Hall of Fame.

I believe everyone actually has two places they were born. The first place is obviously his or her birthplace city. The other is the place where a person begins becoming who they actually are. For me that second place was Dallas. This city gave me a chance more than 40 years ago. To me, Dallas is beautiful, filled with terrific people, very into its sports teams with extremely supportive fans, which is important to me as a sports talk show host for more than 38 years.

I don't really believe there's a uniqueness about Dallas, except that it's more of the New Texas while, just thirty miles away, Fort Worth is more of the Old Texas. Too many people, I think, still remember Dallas as the place where Kennedy was shot. That's fact, and it'll never change. But Dallas has recovered from that to become a fast-growing, vibrant city, one that's becoming a city for international business as well. We have no particular place or part of town that defines us—no French Quarter like New Orleans or Greenwich Village like New York. We're modern, fast-paced. We're a city with lots of "paper businesses," as opposed to manufacturing.

I have been to Houston many times, of course, covering sports. It's very spread out, and it seems to have even more traffic than we do. Is the Ship Channel still occasionally "fragrant"?

JOE NICK PATOSKI

Joe Nick Patoski earned his first set of Texas spurs by going through life with two names—he's invariably "Joe Nick" to his friends and many readers. He earned his second set of spurs writing the world's longest biography of Willie Nelson. Still, his greatest achievement for many has to be his book The Dallas Cowboys: The Outrageous History of the Biggest, Loudest, Most Hated, Best Loved Football Team in America.

Bragging rights are historically based on the performance of the team on the field. In Texas, money is an ever-greater measure of worth.

Titles:

Dallas Cowboys, 1960-Present: Five Super Bowl championships, 10 National Football Conference championships, 21 division championships.

Houston Oilers, 1960-1996: Two American Football League championships, six division championships.

Houston Texans, 2002-Present: Two division championships.

Forbes 2013 value of professional sports franchises:

Dallas Cowboys: $2.3 billion (most valuable in American sports)

Houston Texans: $1.45 billion (5th in the National Football League).

HOUSTON: *Astrodome*

DAN PASTORINI

Born in California, Dan Pastorini came to Houston in 1971 to quarterback the often-hapless Oilers. Under five head coaches over eight years, culminating with Bum Phillips, he and running back Earl Campbell led the franchise to berths in two consecutive AFC playoffs. Today, Pastorini (who grew up in the restaurant business) quarterbacks his own Houston-based seasoning-blend company, DP Quality Foods.

I came to Houston as the Oilers' first draft pick, a small-college kid from a small town, so of course the place seemed huge to me, with something like a million people. Suddenly, I'm in a big city with people expecting some very big things. Our first five years, we lost more games than we won. Trust me, any town is easy to play in when you're winning. Once we actually *did* start winning, the people of Houston started following us and having fun right along with us.

Houston was tough on us at the start, especially since there were so many people here rooting for the Dallas Cowboys. The Oilers were always the "other team" in Texas. When Earl Campbell came along and we started going to the playoffs, people here still liked the Cowboys, but they *loved* us. I remember after losing our first playoff game to our division rivals, the Pittsburgh Steelers—who beat everybody in those days—we flew back to Houston late at night, feeling awful. But then there were 50,000 fans packed in to cheer for us at the Astrodome, in addition to maybe 200,000 lining the route from IAH.

If you remember, we had really unusual team colors: kind of a pastel or powder blue, plus a little bit of red and white. It was about this time that somebody came up with the phrase "Luv Ya Blue," all about our color. We came out on the field for one Monday Night Football game against the Miami Dolphins and we all looked up into the stands together. The place was a sea of powder blue pompoms and placards all saying "Luv Ya Blue." Here in Houston, I still have people come up to me with those placards, crumbling from age. And it makes me feel like those years of playing for the Oilers were special for lots of people in Houston besides me.

Bum Phillips said it all about Houston, which is one of the reasons the city loved him so much. I later played for the Oakland Raiders, the Los Angeles Rams and the Philadelphia Eagles, but there was nothing in those cities like Houston and Bum. He had that blue-collar thing covered. Bum was the greatest coach anybody could ever want to play for. He was no BS and he expected the same from his players and coaches. He was a brilliant defensive strategist, and a whole lot smarter than anybody ever gave him credit for being.

Even though I was long gone, it was rough for me when Bud Adams took his team and moved it to Tennessee, taking the rights to the Oiler name with him. He eventually decided calling his team the Titans would help him get a fresh start there. We always wanted the Oilers here, but he never would let the rights go. I'm happy we have the Texans now, and they're a really talented team. The city has grown. We have four times as many people, enough to fill NRG Stadium every single Sunday. But the loyalty of Texans fans remains to be seen. To replace anything like the Luv Ya Blue years, Texans fans still have a long way to go.

10: SPORTS

LARRY DIERKER

Larry Dierker pitched his first Major League Baseball game on his 18th birthday in 1964, striking out the great Willie Mays. He pitched for the Houston Colt .45s, the Houston Astros and the St. Louis Cardinals and eventually managed the Astros during some of their most successful seasons, 1997-2001. He is the author of two books about baseball, It Ain't Brain Surgery *and* My Team.

I'll never forget seeing the Astrodome for the first time. Darkness had fallen on Houston by the time we got back from spring training in 1965. But as our bus approached, we could see the lights shining right through the roof of the stadium. When we got off the bus we headed for the seats even before we went to the clubhouse. It was breathtaking. I felt as if I had walked into the 21st century. It was like a flying saucer. So colorful; so grand. The scoreboard was huge and it came alive. The home run display was fantastic.

The impression I got of Houston as a sports town evolved over the years. After a few seasons, I got used to the Dome and many of the local fans did, too. Although it was still a marvelous stadium, the novelty wore off. Most Houstonians had *been there and done that*. We still drew well in the summer, when the kids got out of school. But a lot of that was tourism. Astroworld was a new-wave amusement park and it was right across from the Dome. It was a great place to take the family on vacation. But the team itself was average at best during the early years and attendance declined, as you might expect.

What really amped-up the sports scene here was all three professional teams, the Astros, the Oilers and the Rockets becoming play-off teams for the first time in the late 70s and early 80s. I was working in group and season ticket sales and the demand was extraordinary. The oil business was booming at that time, and you didn't have to be a super salesman to sell tickets.

What I see when I go to an Astros game now is often disappointing. At my age, the nature of the experience seems ill suited to the sport. In every stadium and arena these days, the atmosphere is faster-paced, brighter and louder. It's more than just a game. It's loud music, mascots and videos whenever there's even half a minute of downtime. As a kid growing up in Los Angeles in the 1950s, I always heard that baseball was the "national pastime." Lately I've been thinking about what that meant. It's not the "national rage" or the "national frenzy." But it doesn't feel like a pastime either. A lot of people who are good baseball fans would simply like to talk to their friends or read the program between innings. Now with all the marketing hoopla, the game is almost lost in the shuffle.

My biggest personal thrill with the Astros was pitching a no-hitter against the Montreal Expos in 1976, and I'm sure anybody who's ever pitched one would agree. Still, my happiest moment of all was more of a team thing, more of a city thing. All summer long, fans voted for an All-Astrodome All-Star Team and I was chosen as one of the pitchers. It all came down to the last regular season game in the Astrodome in 1999. The all-time team was scheduled to appear on the field after that game. But I was managing the real team that day and we had to win that game to win our division. The post-game ceremony wouldn't have been much fun if we had lost, but we didn't. We won our division for the third straight year. Afterward, all the players stayed on the field, and the fans stayed right there with us for at least half an hour. Confetti was drizzling down from the roof. We were smoking cigars and pouring champagne all over each other. And the fans were part of our joy. That's when the "national rage" seemed appropriate.

BILL BROWN

Missouri-born Bill Brown is a television baseball announcer who has been with the Houston Astros since 1987. He has developed a reputation for being a solid broadcaster and is the author of Houston Astros: Deep in the Heart. *Brown was inducted into the Texas Sports Hall of Fame in 2012, a year after he was inducted into the Media Wall of Honor at Minute Maid Park.*

Houston is a bustling, vibrant city populated by people from all different backgrounds and perspectives. It is a city of immense wealth and also poverty. Its proximity to Mexico has led to a special mix of citizens who speak different languages and have different interests.

But above all, it is a city in which many dreams have been realized and many people have worked together on charity efforts to create a unique blend of cooperation and understanding.

Houston might be thought of by some as a "southern New York City." Most would not find similarities in the two cities, but in the sense that both are "melting pots" of cultures and backgrounds, both bring together diverse interests. The oil and gas worldwide community contributes to the diversity, as does the Port of Houston with its worldwide shipping connections. NASA involves international cooperation and captures the attention of people throughout the world. The academic nature of Rice University, the University of Houston and other educational institutions attracts a tremendous variety of interests and focuses involving the world's citizens. It all fits together into a diverse neighborhood in which people thrive and coexist in a variety of ways.

As the years moved along, there was a natural strengthening of identification for us with Houston. It became "our city" after a time and we became strongly bonded with the city. When the Houston Astros put together their highly successful 2004 and 2005 seasons, it was a pleasure to be identified as one of the broadcasters. In a way I felt that it was a chance to represent the city through publicizing the players and people in the organization and putting the city in a favorable light. It is a responsibility to discuss what the players do for charities in the community and things of that nature, realizing that many sports fans are watching the Astros on television via satellite dish packages as they live in other cities. It is an opportunity to portray some elements of what living in Houston is like to those viewers living elsewhere.

Houston presented me a rare opportunity to be associated with the Astros' success and as a result to be involved in exciting times. The city gained a tremendous reputation for sports and quality of life through playoff games and a World Series. The construction of a new downtown stadium would not have been possible without the team enjoying success on the field.

From the Battle of San Jacinto to modern times, Houston has played a major role in establishing Texas as a unique state. Through its spirit of accomplishment, wildcatters have come in droves to bring oil and gas to the world. Drilling platforms populate the Gulf of Mexico through Houston firms, which have attracted vast capital to finance these ventures. Education has been a major part of the advancement of culture in Houston. The arts have flourished. The sports world has developed. The development of the city by the Allen Brothers put the entire process in motion and allowed the gates to be flung wide open for people with vast dreams to come to Houston and make them reality.

Houston is definitely a city in which dreams turn into concrete accomplishments. The owner of the Houston Astros, Jim Crane, provides one example. A native of St. Louis, Missouri, Jim borrowed $10,000 from a sister to move to Houston and start a shipping company. He bought a truck and started driving it himself and building his business. Eventually it expanded into a worldwide freight company and he acquired other properties, including controlling ownership of the Houston Astros.

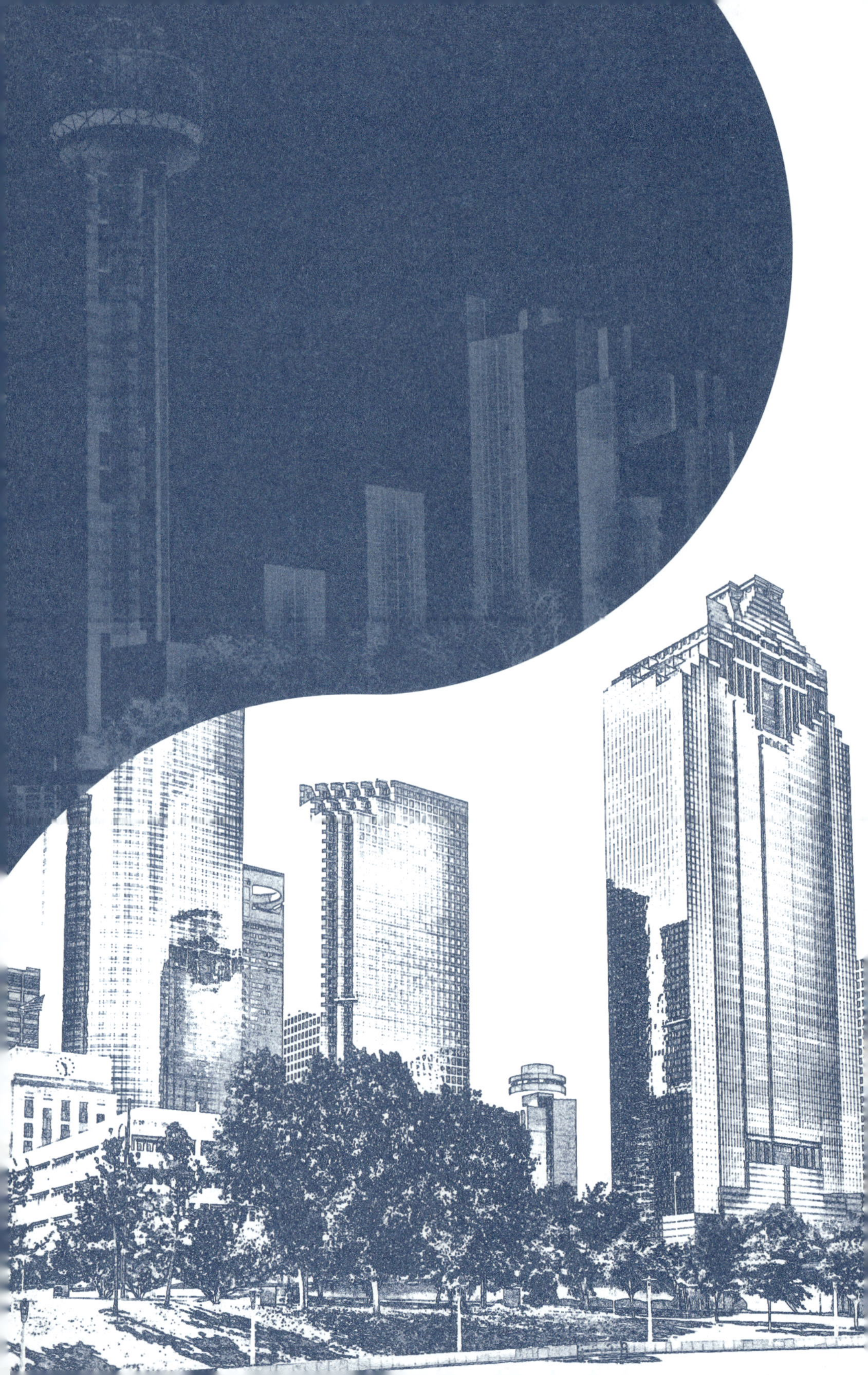

MEDIA

More than virtually any other industry, the media have been transformed, revolutionized, reconstituted and challenged by the steady onslaught of new technology. A business that in the early 1970s still looked and felt much like it did in movies from the 1920s, now it seems to change in some way every six to eight months—each change a life-or-death struggle over the viability of its traditional business model. Daily newspapers, arguably, have been the hardest-hit component of the media, but most of the same challenges confront broadcast television and radio as well. More and more traditional media feature and promote a strong Internet and social media presence, and it's hard not to see this as changing not only their delivery system but also their very reason for being.

Houston and Dallas know media change well, as both cities at one time had at least two thriving daily newspapers and now have only one each. To this day, there are readers in Houston who bemoan the loss of the *Post* and readers in Dallas to wish there were still a *Times-Herald*. At some level, television hangs on to the trappings it introduced decades ago: the trusted anchor (evolved today into a man and a woman engaged in tireless banter) giving the news at the traditional times of day and night. Yet since so many viewers already know what happened from the Internet, TV news, like its print siblings, finds itself either "creating" news through investigative reporting and trying to look deeper behind the headlines.

And then there's radio, now delivered to listeners not only over FCC regulated frequencies but also over computers and smartphones. Once perhaps the most local of all media, charming with a side order of amateur hour, radio has declined in this regard thanks to national conglomerate ownership and now-standard talk-radio and music-format programming. Driving across America, it was possible to experience the strength, diversity and urgency of radio. Now, as the old saying goes, the song remains the same.

JACK SWEENEY

Jack Sweeney was named chairman of the Houston Chronicle *in 2012 after serving as publisher and president since 2000. He began his career with the paper in 1980 as advertising director. Before coming to Houston, Sweeney was the advertising director of the* Boston Herald, *the advertising director of the* Trenton Times *and national automotive manager of the* Washington Post.

For the longest time, in the newspaper business, the goal was to be the only newspaper in town. Here in Houston, we at the *Chronicle* went after the *Post,* and then the *Post* was no more. That meant we had all this wonderful content—innovative reporting, excellent writing—and if readers wanted that content, they had to come to us. So, of course, that meant that local and national advertisers who wanted to reach those readers had to come to us too. As everybody seems to understand by this point, those days are no more.

Still, if we're going to talk about newspapers, we need to start with the things that haven't changed—and that, however many platforms

HOUSTON: *Houston Livestock Show and Rodeo*

we use to deliver what we offer, I hope never will. Sure, if you pick up a printed newspaper today, you can get a lot of those things *without* picking up a newspaper—movie times, the weather forecast, a sports score. What the *Chronicle* alone is doing is getting behind the issues and trying to add some depth to the conversation. Whether it's health care or the pension issue in the city budget, we're looking at things and talking about them in a way that nobody else can. Who else, when it's election time, devotes an editorial board of twelve people to bringing in every single candidate? And talk about being interactive—we had "Letters to the Editor" long before the Internet. Getting people to think is what newspapers do best.

Sometimes, we're all guilty of being too pessimistic about newspapers, here in Houston or in any other big city. The main reason is that we're thinking only of the printed newspaper, as though that exists or can exist in a vacuum anymore. On the one hand, we know there's some kind of chemical reaction between caffeine and ink. A lot of people still like to hold a daily newspaper—their city's daily newspaper—in their hands. But there's so much more to this business now. We need to constantly create new products and train new people to bring them to market. The winners in media are going to be those who let advertisers deliver their products and their values to an audience. It's our job to capture the attention of people who have all these options—print, broadcast, digital and probably options our culture hasn't even thought of yet. There's plenty of ad revenue out there. But unlike in the old days, there are so many ways to spread it around.

And where better to do all this than right here? You hear about Texas and you think big, and then you hear about Houston as the biggest city in Texas. We're the hub of the world's biggest oil and gas industry. We have the world's biggest medical center. Yet on a human level, we have a small-town camaraderie that transcends who you are and where you came here from. It's probably the most diverse city in the country, a city that gets along very well considering the wide range of cultures that live here. It's an easy city to break into—to get involved, to connect.

Have you seen the people selling our advertising these days? They're young, they're smart and they're creative. Trust me, they *have* to be. When I started out in this business, you just had to be that guy with a rate card. Now you have to create programs, ideas, *visions*. You have to help advertisers understand how a package of options can work together to help them deliver their message. And, of course, you have to show them how engaging content about Houston and for Houston can draw together the very people they need to reach.

JEFF GREMILLION

Louisiana-born Jeff Gremillion spent many years writing and editing magazines in New York City before coming "close to home" to serve as founding editor of Houston *magazine. The longest-running presence in each issue's opening pages, Gremillion may be ready to edit out "close to" and simply call Houston home.*

When I first arrived in Houston a decade ago, I remember thinking how weird and unexpected it was that I could do the kind of work I do—running a sophisticated magazine—outside New York. At the time, it felt like I'd won the lottery! I got to do fancy New York-type work, in a town as nice and down-to-earth (and affordable) as Houston! And I could live in a house, with a tree, and not a tiny box, with a mouse! What a difference a decade makes. I now think of Houston, with its amazing growth as a cultural capital and wellspring of economic strength, as the most obvious place in the world to make a chic and glamorous lifestyle periodical.

I love that we are, at the same time, a little bit downhome and folksy, and yet also indisputably urbane and cosmopolitan. Our emergence as a major world city came naturally, because of the things we do and have always done right, not because we emulated another place or tried to position ourselves in some unreal, made-for-TV way. We are just Houston being Houston. And we haven't lost our decent, plain-dealing Texan/Southern *gestalt* in the process. We're like a character actor who just kept on making good movies for years and years before he finally "made it" and became a leading man; by the time the talk shows and tabloids started calling, we were way too set in our ways and assured of our own fundamental worth to let it go to our head.

It's pretty easy to "fit in" in Houston. Or, maybe better said, it's really not all that important that you do fit in. Having good ideas matters more here. Working hard matters more here. Trying to be decent and kind and as generous to others as you can matters more here. A person can make his own persona, his way, and rise to prominence. In many other cities, especially Southern cities, I feel the "who you know factor" is much greater, and I feel, in those other places, that the archetypes of the "successful person" are preordained. Not so in Houston. Perhaps it's unsurprising that a city infamous for having no zoning would have very few rules about who gets to succeed and thrive, and on what terms.

There are too many defining moments in our history to list, of course. But I'll pick one, as an example: The election of Annise Parker. The first openly gay mayor of a major U.S. city. Not New York. Not L.A. Not even San Francisco, for heaven's sake. Houston. And yet it's really not something we ballyhoo around here. There's kind of a "duh" feeling about it. We elected Annise, the well-qualified former controller, not "a lesbian." Her dreams came true, and she rose to greatness here, because she was able to find her own way, create her own unique persona, and sell the rest of us—all also unique, finding our own paths in a city that allows us to—on the idea that she was the right leader at the right time.

Houston is *the* aspirational city of the era. You don't have to have an old family name or stacks of money or a white face or a traditional family arrangement to find your way here and take advantage of the amazing economic and cultural advantages and benefits of the city. The whole world is welcome, and they are coming. And yet, all this "progressiveness" and open-mindedness translate differently here than they do in other progressive cities. We still admire cowboys and folksy wisdom and family dinners after church on Sunday. We maintain a barbecue-loving, bull-riding, God-fearing sense of ourselves, even as we embrace our status as a cosmopolitan, diverse and modern city of the future.

DAVID GOW
Gow Media owns two radio stations and a national radio network, Yahoo! Sports Radio. The company and its owner have done much to promote good causes in Houston over the years, including Literacy Advance and the Center for Hearing and Speech.

In the realm of sports, Houston explodes when it gets a winner. For example, when the Texans make a playoff run, it is really fun to see the banners, flags, t-shirts and enthusiasm all across the city. Notably, there is a rabid, almost paint-your-face nature to the fan base that is, I think, even more over-the-top than what you see with Cowboys fans in Dallas. Houston fans seem more surprised with delight, whereas Dallas fans seem to feel almost entitled to have a winner.

Houston is a welcoming town. We are very ethnically diverse, but without many of the traditional tensions that exist in other cities. In terms of family, this city has provided a great neighborhood and schools for our kids. In terms of faith, we are blessed to participate in a couple of faith-based communities. And in terms of profession, our company has been supported by thoughtful and committed investors. Houston covers all the bases. This is a very entrepreneurial city. There is a powerful combination of optimism and hard work. The mantra: If you believe and work hard, you *will*.

How do you describe a community that can dress up with elegance and yet wear jeans and boots with pride during Rodeo season? Or a community that is a national leader in industries that are as diverse as energy and medicine? And think about energy—it is an Old School industry, yet Houston is an innovator introducing new technologies. Or how do you define a lifestyle that includes our incredible ethnic diversity? I cannot define our lifestyle, and that makes the city all the more compelling.

There is a great culture of philanthropy here. Whether through elegant fundraiser dinners or fun runs, Houstonians are committed to good causes. Also, think of the attractive getaway destinations that are within an hour and a half's drive of Houston—Brenham, Galveston, Magnolia, Trinity and more. All provide a change-of-pace experience. So if you live in Dallas, take heart. Houston is just a few hours away.

LAURETTE VERES
Laurette Veres is editor-in-chief of H Texas *and* Texas Weddings *magazines, and producer of the Bridal Extravaganza Show.*

Houston is extremely prosperous, multicultural and growing. We are the hub of food, fun and entrepreneurship. The diversity is what makes our culture unique. Houston is a very diverse city with an abundance of cultures, producing results that make Houston great. Houstonians are interested in success and celebrating achievement. When local businesses strive, we benefit from their marketing dollars at our magazine. As they succeed, our readership grows. We have been blessed by introducing and reuniting businesses and those who need their products and services.

People with dreams and visions succeed here. And they flock to our coastal city from all over the world to enjoy the entrepreneurial climate. They are drawn here by our state's business-friendly government, the huge pool of qualified professionals from local colleges/universities, an ocean 60 minutes south, champion sports teams, world class dining, shopping offered by every national brand, and great rodeo. The Houston lifestyle is laid back and fun; not pretentious. Both in the suburbs and the city, we enjoy an outdoor lifestyle featuring parks, alfresco dining and abundant cultural events.

A Dallas publisher once told me I could never run a successful city magazine because I did not graduate from a Houston area high school. This sums up the difference between Dallas and Houston. To succeed in Dallas, you have to be from Highland Park. To succeed in Houston, you just have to work hard.

JAMES MORONEY

James M. (Jim) Moroney III has been CEO and director of A. H. Belo Corporation since September 2013 and serves as its president. Mr. Moroney serves as the CEO and publisher at DMNmedia. Moroney has been the CEO and publisher of The Dallas Morning News, Inc., a subsidiary of Belo Corp., since June 2001. He has also served as treasurer at the Newspaper Association of America.

The newsroom of *The Dallas Morning News* is at least three times larger than any other local media newsroom in Dallas. We will be the only local news media organization with the scale to cover local news at a more granular level and do it for the dozen or so separately incorporated municipalities that make up Dallas, Collin, Rockwall and Denton counties. No other local media company has the scale of reporting resources to do this job. In addition, we will continue to do more investigative reporting than any other local news organization, again because we have the scale of newsroom resources to dedicate

DALLAS: *Big Tex-State Fair of Texas*
Photo: *Kevin Brown/State Fair of Texas®*

to enterprise and investigative journalism. We will continue to keep a robust Austin bureau to cover state government. No other local media organization has more than a token presence in Austin today.

The Dallas Morning News is differently positioned than most large metro newspaper companies at present. We have no debt. We have more than $60 million on our balance sheet. We had one of the smallest declines in total revenue among all major metros through the first nine months of this year. This financial condition has allowed us to be entrepreneurial and to experiment: We were the first major metro to systematically begin to raise the price of our home delivered subscriptions and to raise the price of single copy papers (2008). We were the first major metro to put up a so-called paywall and we were among the first to take it down (q1, 2011 and q4, 2013). We were among the first major metros to aggressively acquire commercial printing and distribution contracts (2009) and in q1 of 2104, when we print the *Fort Worth Star-Telegram*, we will print virtually every live edition broadsheet newspaper distributed in the Dallas-Fort Worth area.

The Dallas Morning News continues to help formulate the civic agenda for the city. Certainly there is wider and more diverse participation in formulating and setting the city's agenda than there was twenty and thirty years ago and that's good for the city. Yet through the inevitable changes in leadership at City Hall, in county government and in the c-suite of civically engaged businesses, *The Dallas Morning News,* as an institution, remains committed to the aspiration that Dallas can be the best city in the country.

Today you can read what we publish on desktop and laptops via the traditional web or on iOS and android operating system devices, most notably smartphones and tablets, via the mobile web. We will continue to make what we publish available to consumers when they want it, where they want it, how they want it and on the devices and operating systems of their choices. You have no other choice. You must go where the consumer is. And today, the consumer is increasingly accessing news and information digitally and through mobile. The greatest challenge for newspaper companies it is the challenge to diversity their sources of revenue beyond advertising, both print and digital. Most likely, print will continue to decline and while digital advertising will continue to grow, it will take several more years of declining print ad revenues before the annual growth in digital ad revenue will offset the decline in print ad revenues.

Unless it is a sensational story or the Dallas Cowboys, consumers need to live in North Texas or be a loyal ex-pat to want to consume what we publish daily. So at low rates and without huge scale, you can't pay for the scale of newsrooms that newspaper companies presently employ without other sources of revenue. The hope comes from the fact that people are always interested in news and information that is relevant to their lives. This fact won't change.

HAL JAY

The most recognizable laugh in the Metroplex belongs to Fort Worth native Hal Jay, host of the WBAP Morning News from 5 to 9 a.m. A key member of the WBAP team since 1981, Hal started his broadcast career in Liberal, Kansas, and worked at stations in Fort Worth and Memphis before joining WBAP.

I've had this same laugh for years, since I was a kid really, this wheezy, cartoony kind of laugh. I think that when I laugh on the air it sounds like I have emphysema. But when I go places and meet people, they often ask me to just go ahead and laugh for them. It's a very nice compliment for that to happen.

I think of Dallas as a highly competitive media market. It's a big market, since all of the major networks own stations here, both radio and television. But it's also a market where people tend to come and settle in and like it. There doesn't seem to be much turnover when it comes to media here, whether on the air talent or off the air, but especially on. Even people who move from station to station try to stay in the Dallas-Fort Worth market. They like the area. And it's not for the 105 degrees in the summertime.

The secret in almost any business is longevity. You just have to keep doing it over and over. If people keep waking up to the same voice on the radio or the same face on television year after year, what you're telling them feels more dependable. I guess some people in this business still want to move to New York or Los Angeles or

Chicago, but I've been offered jobs in all those markets and have turned them all down. Dallas is a great place to live, especially if you have a family. And once you do have one, you think a little bit more about it than about building your resume.

Every town has its bad guys of course, but in the big picture I think Dallas people are very friendly. And the economy has never tanked here. It went down somewhat during the recession, but it always stayed pretty solid. Dallas doesn't have a coast and it doesn't have any mountains, but overall it's a nice place to settle down. There are great things to see and do in the arts districts of both Dallas and Fort Worth, and the museums are unbelievable. The zoos are great too. These cities have everything anybody could want as a family.

For the most part, being an anchor of the WBAP news operation, I've been studio-bound, but if I wanted to go out and cover a particular story I certainly could. My biggest memory to this day is being on the air talking about how a small plane had just crashed into the Twin Towers in New York City. And all the time I was talking, I was looking at the video they were playing on TV and thinking there was no way a small plane had caused that kind of damage. That was 9/11. And then all hell broke loose.

People in Dallas have listened to my sons, Josh and Carter, pretty much grow up on the air, and now they're 33 and 30. And they know all about my wife Ann. My son signed a full scholarship to TCU on the air. The audience feels almost like they're part of our family because I'm talking about things that are personal in my life, and making them somewhat public. I guess wherever you go, but especially here in Dallas, people like to listen to somebody they feel like they know.

ROSE-MARY RUMBLEY

Rose-Mary Rumbley could be described as a Renaissance Woman: humorist, teacher, actress, historian, journalist and author. Her published books include such page-turners as Dear Santa–Thanks for the Piano; The Unauthorized History of Dallas; Dallas, Too *and* What? No Chili: Meet Hot Shot and Visit Food Festivals over Texas.

My great-grandparents arrived in Dallas in 1865 with their four girls, one of them being my grandmother, who grew up in Dallas and married a baker. My grandfather opened the Westend Bakery on Main Street, in 1880, and my blessed mother was born in 1894 in the living quarters over the bakery. Mother lived all of her 90 years in Big D and she told stories about all that she had seen—the changes, the improvements, and the discoveries. I was born in Dallas, a proud fourth-generation Dallasite.

People like my great-grandparents came to Dallas to start businesses, and some were new and innovative. A large number of Jewish merchants came to this area and opened stores that eventually gained international fame—to name one, Neiman Marcus. Then oil was discovered in Texas and Magnolia Oil chose Dallas as the headquarters with a skyscraper, topped by a Flying Red Horse. Later, a bunch of geniuses gathered in a shack and came up with microchips—Texas Instruments. Edwin Doolin stirred some cornmeal and made Fritos. There are many other unique success stories coming from Dallas.

In 1936, Texas was 100 years old. The cry of the day: Let's Celebrate! Where? A meeting was called with all the big cities of Texas represented. The party (it was said) should be in Houston, where Sam Houston defeated the Mexican Army and declared Texas a Republic. Wait! There is the Alamo, cradle of Texas liberty. The party should be in San Antonio. Wait! Stephen F. Austin came first and founded his little colony on the Colorado River. The party should be in our state's capital, Austin. Fort Worth was not represented at the meeting but R.L. Thornton, mayor of Dallas, was there. "We have no history in Dallas, but here's $10 million in cash. The party is in Dallas!"

Some of our friends in Austin wear T-shirts: KEEP AUSTIN WEIRD. I have a T-shirt: KEEP DALLAS PRETENTIOUS. Of course, there are a few snobs here, but most of all, there are fine "salt of the earth people."

Dallas has more Book Review Clubs than any other city in the nation. This is a proven fact. A charming woman by the name of Ermance Rejebian came to Dallas with her husband from Armenia in the 1920s, and she told of the horrors that happened in Armenia after World War I. People were fascinated by her stories, so much so that review clubs were organized to hear what she had to say. These clubs are still meeting. I speak to them all. Of course, a favorite topic is Dallas. I am billed as the "one who knows everything about Dallas." Thank you, mother. She's the one who gave me the material. I know she would be proud.

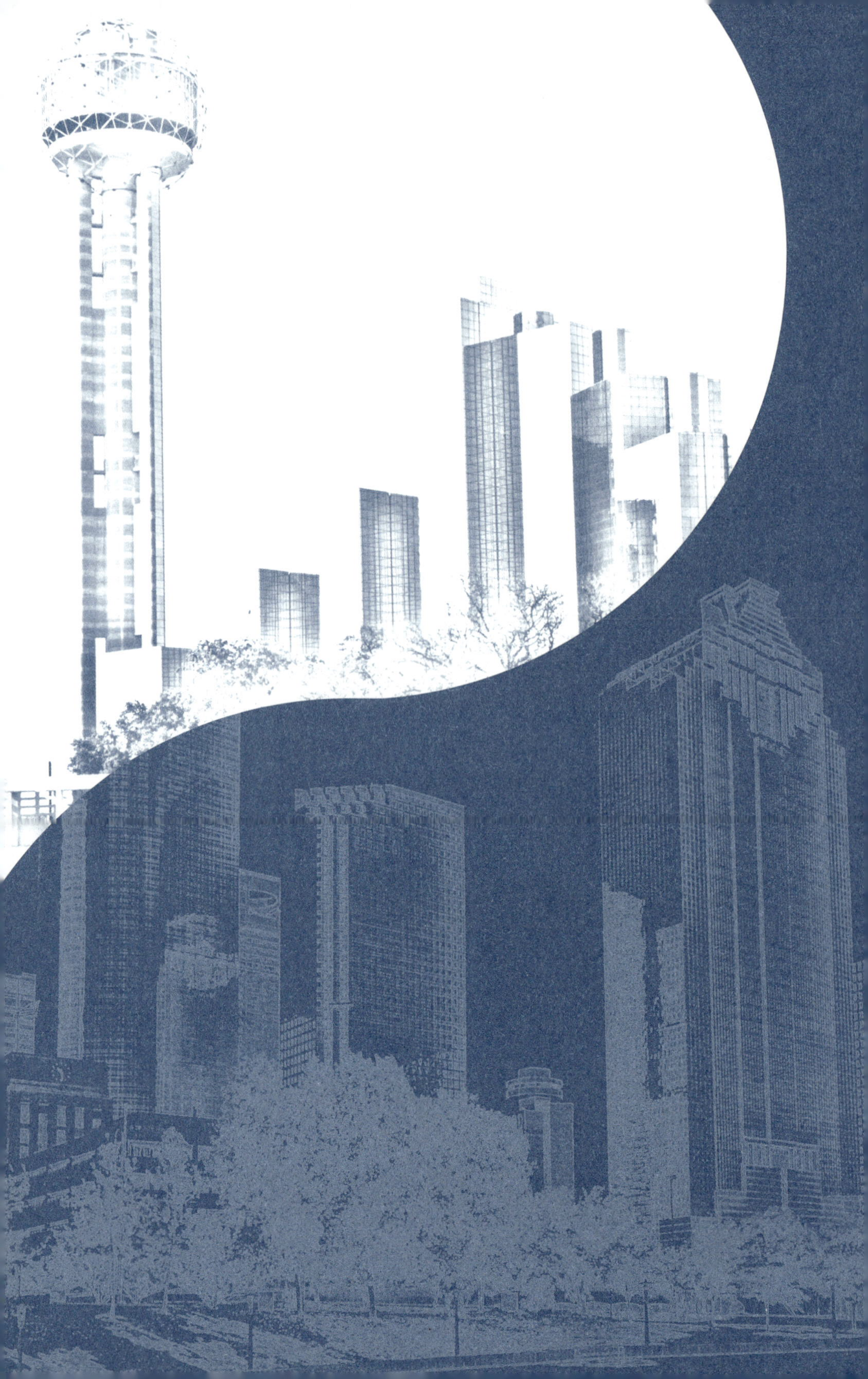

THE PROMISE
THE FUTURE OF DALLAS & HOUSTON

―――――――――

LYNN ASHBY

What will Dallas and Houston look like in 20 or 50 or 100 years? Who will live there, what will they look like, how will they commute, will the two Texas towns finally be on speaking terms, will the Texans ever beat the Cowboys again? We left our tale of two cities at the year 2000, a good benchmark, when it appeared there was nothing to stop both Dallas and Houston galloping forward, but not all for the better. In the future, certainly there will be more people. They will occupy more space, hold down more jobs (and want more jobs), have more babies and have more funerals. On the other hand, they will generate more garbage and pollution, flush more toilets and fill more jail cells.

Let's back up and look at all of Texas. The 2010 Census shows that Latinos accounted for two-thirds of the state's growth over the previous decade. They now make up 38% of the Texas population, up from 32% in 2000. The Anglo population has now dropped to 45.3%, down from 52.4% in 2000. About 11.5% of the population is black, unchanged from 10 years earlier. Almost all of the state's future population growth is expected to occur in just four areas: Houston-Galveston, Dallas-Fort Worth, the Austin-San Antonio corridor and the lower Rio Grande Valley.

Ever since the very first census in 1790, New York City has been the most populous city in America. Every other city and has changed places in the pecking order—next, in that first census, came Philadelphia and Boston. No surprises there, but then came Charleston, South Carolina, followed by Baltimore, Northern Liberties, Salem, Newport, Providence and Marblehead. For the next 50 years Northern Liberties was among our largest populated cities. Texas wasn't around back then.

Today Texas is the only state with three cities in the top 10, but even among the three, the order keeps changing. Mike Cox, in his syndicated column, "Texas Tales," determined in the first U.S. Census of Texans, in 1850, the enumerators found 212,592 people in the state, including slaves but not Indians. The top 10 looked like this: Galveston (4,177), San Antonio (3,488), Houston (2,396), New Braunfels (1,723), Marshall (1,180), Gonzales (1,072), Victoria (802), Fredericksburg (754), Austin (629), Corpus Christi (533). Four different cities have been number 1 in the state: Galveston, San Antonio and Dallas once (1890). Houston took over in 1930 and has been there ever since. Dallas is an interesting case. It finally broke in as 9th biggest in Texas in 1860, right behind Sulphur Springs. By 1880 Big D was still smaller than Austin, yet—as noted earlier—within 10 years, 1890, Dallas was briefly the biggest city in Texas. Today it has been surpassed by San Antonio, and Austin is gaining.

The 2010 census found that 2,099,451 people lived in the city of Houston proper. (A 2011 estimate put it at 2,145,146.) The census counted 4,092,459 in Harris County and 5,946,800 in that 10-county region. Harris County, which grew by 20.3% since 2000, is the 3rd largest county in population nationally, behind Los Angeles and Cook

(Chicago) counties. New York City is comprised of several counties or boroughs—Brooklyn, Manhattan, etc. By 2024, without immigration, the population of Harris County is expected to be about 4.3 million, only a slight increase. (The Houston-Galveston Area Council has forecasted that the Houston region alone will grow by 3.5 million people in the next few decades.) If the past rate of growth is any indication, by 2040 Harris County is expected to be 6.8 million, a 70% increase or almost 1.8% growth per year. The 10-county region is expected to grow even faster, from 6 to over 11 million. Between 2000 and 2006 the population of Harris County increased by 485,653. It is as though every man, woman and child in pre-Katrina New Orleans moved there, and sometimes it seems they have. However, many of the newcomers moved here from the North. Do you ever get the idea that the Border Patrol is watching the wrong river?

According to Peter Bishop, an associate professor of Strategic Foresight and coordinator of the graduate program in Futures Study at the University of Houston, demographers work with three "Houstons"—the City of Houston, Harris County, and the Houston-Sugar Land-Baytown metro area. Bishop notes that projections show Houston's population on average will be older. The county is currently a little more than 25% under 18 (children), 65% 18-64 (adult) and 7.5% over 65 (retired). By 2040, the proportion of children will drop to 20%, and the proportion of older people will just about double to 13%. That is higher than the proportion of older people in Florida today, Bishop observes.

On the other hand, Dallas, with a population density per square mile of 2,718, is packed into 340,519 square miles and can't grow unless it takes over one of its surrounding suburbs. Houston's size is an interesting story. Like the Texas rancher said, "I ain't greedy. All I want is my own land and that next to it." The Legislature gave the Bayou City Extra-Territorial Jurisdiction or ETJ, which is essentially a five-mile band around the city's general-purpose boundaries, with the exception of instances when that band intersects another municipality or its own ETJ. Some night you will hear a big bang when Houston and San Antonio collide near Columbus.

Dallas ranks 9th among American cities in population with 1,197,816 in the 2010 U.S. Census, an increase of only .78% in 10 years. (In that same period, San Antonio counted 1.3 million people, up by 16%.) But the actual population of the city of Dallas is misleading. It is totally surrounded by other municipalities, thus most of the population growth is outside the city limits, a situation made worse by the white flight. A more accurate picture is changes in the county and those surrounding it. In the 2010 census, Dallas County held 2,368,139 residents while a 2012 estimate put the figure at 2,453,843. A quick measure of the two sprawling areas is that the Metroplex is the nation's 5th largest TV market and Houston is the 10th, so it costs more to advertise on TV in Dallas than in Houston.

Everyone in both cities is from somewhere else. Two quick examples: On autumn Saturdays the word is out, even sometimes posted in the newspapers, where college alumni will meet to watch their alma mater play football. LSU, OU, Vanderbilt and others have large contingents in both cities. Then check the newspaper obituaries. "Charles Jones was born in Chicago and came to Dallas to work for Texas Instrument." "Gloria Smith, born in Los Angeles, was transferred to Houston by Exxon in 1983." Indeed, it is a point of pride to include "native Texan" or "a second generation Houstonian" because it is somewhat rare.

THE CHANGING FACE OF TEXAS

What will Houstonians look like in the future? By 2012, Harris County was already 41% Hispanic, 32% Anglo, 19% African-American and 8% Asian or other, and is heading for a majority Hispanic population around 2015. By 2040, almost 7 of 10 residents of Harris County will be Hispanic. Even including the outlying counties, which have more Anglos, the region will be majority Hispanic by 2040. The area also has a growing Asian population, complete with Vietnamese members in the City Council and the Texas Legislature, two Chinese daily newspapers and some great Asian restaurants. The percentage of blacks seems to stay the same in recent headcounts and shows no sign of that percentage growing.

Stephen Klineberg, a Rice sociology professor who has been chronicling Houston for decades in his Houston Area Survey, says Houston's population growth in the 60s and 70s up until 1982 consisted of Anglos pouring into the city. Since the collapse of the oil industry in 1982, it's been all non-Anglo. He is often quoted as saying this multi-racial city has become one of the most culturally diverse cities in the nation. "The Houston Area Survey reveals that, of all the 60-plus population, 67.3% are Anglo. Under the age of 30, more than 75% of Houstonians are non-Anglo. There is no force in the world that is going to stop Houston from becoming more Latino and more Asian." Klineberg points out that the Houston ISD has 200,000 students of which 61.7% are Latino, and 26.5% are African American. "Of both populations, 45% drop out of high school. Both factions are overwhelmingly living in poverty, as seen by the fact that more than 79% qualify for reduced-cost and free lunch programs."

A quick way to note Houston's internationalism is that it has more than 80 foreign consulates, a count only behind those of Washington and New York City. Immigration experts say that people who move to a new city or even to a new country for good often simply follow a friend or relative who moved there before and recommends the place. It's a snowball effect. Like Houston and the rest of Texas, Dallas' Latino population is booming, up 20% between 2000 and 2010, from 35 to 42% of the total. As a result, there is a healthy Hispanic presence in Big D, including Spanish language radio and TV stations, plus publications. Some of the suburbs have tried to limit this growth: Farmers Branch tried to pass an ordinance preventing the renting of houses to illegal immigrants, but courts keep denying it.

HOUSTON OR DALLAS? DALLAS OR HOUSTON?

To compare Houston and Dallas, *Forbes* magazine rated Houston the "coolest city in America." This was based on entertainment, restaurants, bars and job growth. Dallas finished 4th, San Antonio 11th and Fort Worth 13th. Oddly enough, the People's Republic of Austin barely made the top 20 at 19th. *Forbes* also ranked Dallas as second among U.S. cities in the number of billionaires, with 17. Houston finished 7th, with 11. Five Texas malls are among the 50 biggest shopping malls in America: The Houston Galleria is 9th largest. North Park Center in Dallas ranks 19th. Actually, Texas has three more in the top 50 in America: Brazos Town Center, Rosenberg—(30th), Memorial City Mall, Houston (38th) and North East Mall, Hurst (47th). Number

1 is the Mall of America in Bloomington, Minnesota. Houston has a Theater District second only to New York City with its concentration of seats in one geographic area. Dallas has the State Fair of Texas.

There is one great difference in the unofficial running of the two cities. The movers and shakers in Dallas often don't actually live in the city of Dallas. Robert L. Thornton built and lived in a home in Highland Park, on the corner of Cornell and Auburndale. When Thornton was elected president of one of the major banks in downtown Dallas, the bank's directors said he should live in the city of Dallas, so he sold his house to the bank and moved within the city limits of Dallas. His house stood empty for six months, (someone threw a brick through a large picture window in the front and rainfall swelled the wooden floors inside) until my father bought the place, which had large T's-for-Thornton in the front grill.

It was famed racing driver and Houstonian A.J. Foyt who once observed, "I feel safer on a racetrack than I do on Houston's freeways." That gives us an idea of what it's like to drive on the freeways, and there are a lot of them: 1,835 lane miles in the county. To quote George Greanias, former head of Houston's Metro: "One thing's for sure: More people are moving to Houston." He urges that the area stay ahead of the curve in transportation. According to Greanias, every dollar invested in public transportation generates approximately $6 in economic returns. But the Bayou City lags far behind most American cities in mass transit, mostly because of the town's three amigos: Former Mayor Bob Lanier, former Congressman Tom DeLay and current U.S. Representative John Culberson. For reasons known only to them, they successfully stymied most efforts to build heavy or even light rail to make it in Houston, once even sending $45 million in federal transportation funds earmarked for Houston to—get this—Dallas. This brings us to Houston's sleek subway system—of which there is none. Early Houston had an excellent mass transit system until the mule died. Today Houstonians consider "mass transit" taking their 12-seat Dodge Exterminator to church.

If you look at an early map of Houston you will see rail lines branching out from downtown like spokes on a wheel. Indeed, for years the city's motto was: "Where 23 railroads meet the sea," which must have made a terrible splash. The rail lines were perfect rights-of-way for light or heavy rail. One by one the rails were ripped up and paved over. According to the Texas Transportation Institute, Houston is the 6th most-congested city in the nation. In 2012 the average Houstonian wasted 23 gallons of gas sitting in traffic. Drivers in that area wasted more than two days a year on average in traffic congestion, costing them nearly $1,100 in lost time and gas. Dallas didn't even make the top 10.

Mass transit can mean more personal savings and a smaller environmental impact for Houstonians. The American Public Transportation Association reports that public transportation saves individuals, on average, $9,656 a year. And if a single commuter switches to public transportation, he or she can reduce household carbon emissions by 10%—or up to 30% if the household eliminates a second car. A not insignificant impact on the city's vehicle increase is pollution. All those additional vehicles belching smoke into an August afternoon will do bad things to Houstonians' lungs.

The Houston area ranked number one in the nation in exports for 2012, for the first time: $110.3 billion surpassing NYC's $102 billion. The Dallas-Fort Worth-Arlington area ranked 8th with $27.8 billion. Transportation experts predict movement of goods by rail and water will grow rapidly in the next several years. Combined, trucks, trains and ships moved 930 million tons of freight worth $1.6 trillion during 2007 in the eight-county Houston area. By 2035, 1.5 billion tons of freight worth $3.4 trillion is projected to traverse local highways, rail lines and waterways. Trucks are the main mode of travel for goods, though pipelines carry much of the region's valuable cargo. Excluding pipelines, trucks carry about half the commodities into and out of the Houston region, around 465 million tons based on 2007 data. That figure is expected to grow to 781 million tons by 2035, the planners say. The increase could be devastating. Based on semi-tractor trailer loads of 25 tons, roughly what the normal 53-foot rig carries, the number of trips needed would go from 18.6 million in 2007 to 31.2 million in 2035. We only have to look at what the heavy trucks are doing to south Texas roads involved in the fracking boom to see what could be ahead for the Houston region.

DART, the Dallas area mass transit system, is working on 90 miles of light rail serving 62 stations, while Houston in late 2014 will have 22 miles of track and 38 major stops. In February of 2014, Houston had a little more than one-seventh Dallas' track mileage and almost half as much ridership. In Dallas, with 85 miles of track, DART logged almost 2.2 million trips in February. Metro recorded 1.03 million trips on 12.8 miles.

Here is an excellent comparison by Tory Gattis, a social systems architect with Open Model Consulting in Houston: "The Brookings Institution had already confirmed Houston as one of most upwardly mobile urban areas of the country after the city saw a 48% reduction in hard-core poverty in the 1990s. The mobility plan also came just in the nick of time to save Houston from following Dallas into fragmentation and stagnation. In 2004, a *Dallas Morning News* special report noted that employers were fleeing to suburban cities and counties, in part because their suburban family employees couldn't easily get into the city, leaving Dallas with the highest downtown vacancy rate in the nation and a declining commercial tax base. It was the ever-dreaded Detroit scenario: a declining core in a thriving metro. Dallas had succeeded with light rail and dense, urban development, but residents were facing declining employment options along the rail lines. In contrast, Houston, by providing a strong mix of freeways, express arterials, commuter transit and light rail, was able to keep its employers in the core with easy access by both their suburban and urban employees.

When it comes to air traffic, Big D is far superior. Dallas and its Sancho Panza to the west, Fort Worth, share DFW Airport which rules the Southwest in air travel. DFW covers 26.9 square miles and is larger than Manhattan. It is the 4th in the world in operations and 8th in passengers. In 2011 that would be 57,806,918 embarrassing body scans. But note that Dallas has not produced anyone important enough to carry its airport's name. Houston has the George H.W. Bush Intergalactic Airport & Bait Camp that handled 40,187,442 passengers in 2011 making the airport the 10th busiest for total passengers in North America and 17th busiest on Earth. It covers 17.1875 square miles which is not the size of Manhattan. When travelers go from Houston's Mickey Leland Complex to Love Field, do they realize both were named for people who died in plane crashes? It gives air travel a whole new meaning for the word "terminal."

In the summer of 2014 yet another plan was trotted out for high-speed rail between Dallas and Houston. This rail route is nothing new. In the early 20th Century there were trains leaving several times a day from each city headed for the other. (My grandfather started his railroad career as a conductor on that line.) Gov. Rick Perry proposed his famous Texas Triangle high-speed rail plan which included Austin/San Antonio. Others have made the same proposal. This latest plan is a privately funded $10 billion project to begin construction in 2016. Good luck.

CHALLENGES

Restaurants in the Metroplex could well put up signs in their restrooms: "Please flush—Houston needs the water." According to a National Academy of Sciences study, during summers almost all of the Trinity River, which is Houston's main water supply, is wastewater discharged from Dallas and Fort Worth. There must be a lot of flushing going on because Houston is fortunate to have ample water supply due to lakes formed by damming the aforementioned Trinity River. But in future years the fast-growing Metroplex will be wanting more of that water, and there is talk of tapping the Trinity by the booming Georgetown-Austin-San Marcos corridor. Both Dallas and Houston face enormous growths in population, which means more vehicles belching out more pollutants. Adding to Houston's air quality is one of the world's largest petro-chemical complexes, and smog is a certainty in the future unless strong measures are taken, which currently looks unlikely.

There is probably a maxim that freeways are overcrowded the day they open. How much concrete can be poured? This brings Houston, more so than Dallas, to another problem. To the west and north of the city large plots of open ground are being covered over with concrete streets, shopping center, houses, more freeways, and yet the rainfall doesn't dwindle, and it all runs down the bayous, through the city and into the Gulf. Where to put all that water? As for trash, the average American generates 4.6 pounds of garbage each day. Landfills are already filling up, and not with land. Unless both metropolitan areas start planning, they are facing a desperate hunt for more dumps. Perhaps Arkansas.

Houstonians would probably not like to compare professional sports teams of the past. The Dallas Cowboys, Stars, Mavericks and the Texas Rangers have all won national championships. The Houston Rockets have won two NBA championships, while the Houston Astros have played in one world series and lost every game. Much was made, at least in Houston, when the Astros switched to the American League and an "I-45 rivalry" was touted. So far it hasn't developed and, unless Houston's boys of summer improve greatly, it never will. Brand Keys, a marketing company, polled fans to see how exciting a team is during competition; how well they play as a team; how well respected and admired the players are; and the extent to which the game and the team are part of a fans' and community's rituals, institutions and beliefs. Which baseball teams have the most loyal fans? The New York Yankees finished first. At the very bottom, at number 30, were the Houston Astros, down from number 23 the year before.

Houston is the largest city in the nation without zoning, which gives its residents the convenience of building a multi-million dollar mansion and seeing a tattoo parlor built next door. There are neighborhood restrictions, but they don't help if a developer has deep pockets and a good lawyer. Zoning may come along some day, probably by another name. Dallas has zoning. The two downtowns continue to fight for relevance. Getting people to move to the downtown has always been a hot topic—lofts come and go in popularity. Yet other cities are having far more success in this pursuit.

Dallas' future, like that of Houston, will see a continued growth in population and all its pleasures and problems, but the city of Dallas itself, unlike its neighbor to the south, will be the key, dependent on nearby towns. There is already some regional government, yet Big D may follow the example of Miami and Dade County which is Miami-Dade County, a "two tier system." Expect to see Dallas, Fort Worth, Arlington and all the other nearby towns joined in one vast, controlling governmental body.

If a newcomer to Texas was trying to decide whether to live in Dallas or Houston, based on which has the best public schools for the children, you might give the pilgrim a comparison. The Dallas

ISD has an enrollment of 157,575 and 70 languages spoken, while the Houston ISD's enrollment is 201, 927 and has 95 languages spoken. TEEP (Teacher Effectiveness Enhancement Programme) has listed the top 100 high schools for Texas:

#1 by TEEP is DISD's School for Gifted and Talented
#3 is DISD's School of Science and Engineering
#5 is DeBakey High School for Health Professions—HISD
#6 is Highland Park High School in the HPISD
#7 is Carnegie Vanguard—HISD

The need for additional public schools is obvious, although more and more parents who can afford it are putting their children in private and parochial schools. Community colleges also face huge enrollment increases, which can be handled a lot easier than Rice, the University of Houston, SMU and the smaller institutions can cope with growing student bodies.

Apartment Guide looked at its data on the top cities for keeping cool in the summer, with apartment listings that included AC units, community pools on property and ceiling fans. Houston was 7th. Dallas didn't make the top 10. (Tulsa was number 1.) Upon graduation, many college students feel it's time to move on. Indeed, 70% in a recent poll said they planned on changing cities. Apartment Guide looked at moving patterns and has identified the top "sister metros"—or where people most often move from and where they move to. Moving from Dallas to Houston was 7th. Among the top searched metros,— i.e., cities that were investigated as possible new homes—Dallas was 3rd and Houston was 4th. CBS did a survey to find the Top 10 Moving Destinations. Number 2 was Dallas. Number 6 was Houston. The Fortune 500 ranked the largest American companies. Texas had 25, and of those 20 in the Dallas or Houston environs—Houston had 11, Dallas had 9.

Since 2007, the state's Smoking Vehicle Program has received nearly 60,000 complaints from citizens about cars or trucks emitting excessive smoke on the roads of Texas. Houston leads all cities with 15,300 complaints, followed by San Antonio, which reported nearly 11,000, and Austin, with 9,400. Dallas ranked 4th with 1,945, but there is also the North Central Texas Council of Governments that runs a separate program, and some complaints have gone there. On the other hand, in a recent ranking, Houston—with its sprawling interstates, highways and toll roads—came out on top of other large Texas cities as a "walkable." Dallas was No. 30 and Austin was No. 31. New York, San Francisco and Boston took the top three spots in the ranking.

BRAGGING RIGHTS

Where do we go from here? There is plenty here to boost either city's backers, especially if they cherry-pick some facts and ignore the rest. And there is much that each city might want from the other—would Houston trade NASA for the State Fair? Does Dallas covet the international flavor of Houston? Would the Bayou City prefer Big D's climate?

We have seen the exciting and colorful history of each place, the present, and what lies ahead (more excitement). They have their similarities and distinct individualism. Oddly, these two Texas towns that share so much, including the Texas Legislature, don't communicate with each other very often. Not many residents have much to do with the other city. Example: While morning flights by Southwest Airlines fly scores of lawyers carrying their black leather briefcases to do business in the other city, they also fly the lawyers back home at night.

Our survey of leaders in both communities shows civic pride, but a reluctance to comment on the gathering at the other end of I-45. Their mommas done taught them well. And why bash the other guy when there is so much going on just outside? Joel Kotkin, an urbanologist based in California, says all signs point to three North American cities to be the future—*Calgary, Dallas and Houston.* Two out of three ain't bad. If the past is prologue to the future, let's get together in a few decades and see how this tale of two cities pans out. Until then, whether you are in Dallas or Houston, buy land.

SOURCES

Brennan, Morgan, *Coolest Cities*, Forbes, July 26, 2012.

Cox, Mike, *Texas Tales* (syndicated column), www.texasescapes.com

CNN Money, *Annual Ranking of America's Largest Corporations*, Texas, 2012.

Durgy, Edwin, *Cities with the most Forbes 400 Members*, Forbes, September 22, 2011.

Gattis, Tory, *www.houstonstrategies.com*

Glink, Ilyce, *Top 10 Moving Destinations*, CBS Money Watch, January 28, 2013.

Greanias, George, *Houston Metro: Traffic Woes and Mass Transit*, Houston PBS, September 24, 2010, www.support.houstonpbs.org

Greater Houston Partnership, *Greater Houston Region Named #1 Metro by SITE Selection Magazine For 2ND Year in a Row*, March 4, 2013, https://www.houston.org/economic-development/ratings-rankings index.

Greater Houston Partnership, *Houston Facts*, www.houston.org

H Texas magazine.

Hines, Andy & Bishop, Peter, *Thinking about the Future. Guidelines for Strategic Foresight*. Washington DC: Social Technologies, LLC, 2006.

Houston Chronicle

http://www.houstontx.gov/abouthouston/houstonfacts.html "Houston Facts and Figures." July 7, 2014.

Kotkin, Joel, *World Capitals of the Future*, Forbes, September 2, 2009.

Office of Economic Development, City of Dallas, *Dallas Economic Development and Accolades*, www.ecodev.org

Rice University Kinder Institute for Urban Research, *Houston Area Survey on Health, Education, and Arts (SHEA)*, Todd C. Litton of Citizen Schools Texas.

Rice University Shell Center for Sustainability, *Workshop on Houston's Future: Trends, Challenges and Scenarios*, December 2004.

Rudick, Tyler. "All Aboard! 205 MPH Bullet Train between Houston and Dallas is closer than ever," Culture Map. January 9, 2014.

Teacher Effectiveness Enhancement Programme, TEEP Top 100 High Schools, www: teep.tamu.edu/complete rankings.

Texas State Historical Society, *Handbook of Texas*.

The Center for Houston's Future, www.centerforhoustonsfuture.org

The City of Houston: *Facts and Figures*.

The Dallas Morning News, *Texas Almanac*.

The Houston-Galveston Area Council

The Houston Post

Thomson, Steve, *Rice Professor Stephen Klineberg Predicts Houston's Ethnic Future*, Imagine Houston's Future (Editorial Special Series), Culture Map, February 7, 2011.

U.S. Census Bureau

Young, S.O., *A Thumbnail History of The City of Houston, Texas*, Ingleside, TX: Compano Bay Press, Trade Edition, 2010.

www.thedallasartdistrict.org, January 26, 2009.